THE IP MIRACLE

THE IP MIRACLE

HOW TO TRANSFORM IDEAS INTO ASSETS THAT MULTIPLY YOUR BUSINESS

JiNan Glasgow George
Durham, NC

This book is for informational purposes only. It is not intended to serve as a substitute for professional legal advice. The author and publisher specifically disclaim any and all liability arising directly or indirectly from the use of any information contained in this book. A qualified legal professional should be consulted regarding your specific situation. Any product mentioned in this book does not imply endorsement of or affiliation with that product by the author or publisher.

The conversations in the book are based on the author's recollections, though they are not intended to represent verbatim transcripts. Rather, the author has retold them in a way that communicates the spirit of what was said. While select Neo IP clients appear in this book with permission, other examples and stories featured throughout the book are inspired by true events but have been anonymized and/or pseudonymized to retain the spirit of what occurred. In several instances, identifying names and details have been altered to protect anonymity and to maintain confidentiality.

JiNan Glasgow George
P.O. Box 52546
Durham, NC 27717
www.neoipassets.com
Send feedback to book@neoipassets.com

Publisher's Cataloging-In-Publication Data

   Names: George, JiNan Glasgow, author.
   Title: The IP miracle : how to transform ideas into assets that multiply your business / JiNan Glasgow George.
   Description: Durham, NC : JiNan Glasgow George, [2022] | Includes bibliographical references.
   Identifiers: ISBN 9798985562507 (hardcover) | ISBN 9798985562514 (softcover) | ISBN 9798985562521 (ebook)
   Subjects: LCSH: Intellectual capital. | Intellectual property. | Assets (Accounting) | Business enterprises--Valuation. | Success in business.
   Classification: LCC HD53 .G46 2022 (print) | LCC HD53 (ebook) | DDC 658.4063--dc23

Special discounts for bulk sales are available.
Please contact book@neoipassets.com.

To God, who gives us the unlimited resource of ideas;
to my family, who love and support me in all things;
to my team at Neo IP and Patent Forecast, who collaborate
to create positive impact every day;
and to my clients, who give us the privilege of helping them
transform their ideas into assets to make a positive impact in
the world.

Contents

Tell Me What You Think

Let other readers know what you thought of *The IP Miracle*. Please write an honest review for this book on your favorite online bookshop.

Want someone to implement the lessons of *The IP Miracle* for you?

Author JiNan Glasgow George is the founder of Neo IP, an intellectual property law firm with a holistic approach to creating Intellectual Property (IP) assets.

JiNan and her team believe Intellectual Property is a valuable business asset with exceptional potential. Filing a patent is a relatively small cost for the asset you're creating, and it multiplies the value of your current assets and the business overall.

If you don't protect your ideas, someone might steal them from you. That doesn't mean you should file patents or register trademarks "just in case." Leveraged properly, IP, can protect your business and exponentially increase its value.

If you have any questions about IP or would like help filing yours, reach out to Neo IP today.

www.neoipassets.com

CHAPTER 1

IDEAS ARE ASSETS

66 **I**ntellectual property law doesn't really apply to me."
Do you believe that? In my experience, most business owners and founders do. I've worked with clients on their intellectual property (IP) for over twenty years, and one of my greatest challenges is convincing entrepreneurs that what they *know* has tangible, measurable value.

You could be sitting on a gold mine and not even realize it. And if you don't protect it, someone else may steal it from you. That doesn't mean you should file patents or register trademarks "just in case." IP is not insurance. It's an asset class of its own. And leveraged properly, IP can bring you prosperity beyond your wildest dreams.

• • • •

When you think of concrete, your next thought probably isn't about gunfire. Yet that's how this story goes. One of my clients at my IP law firm, Neo IP, is a family concrete company. The owner, Bob, is an older, salt-of-the-earth man with weathered hands and concrete under his fingernails. He's a walking encyclopedia entry on concrete materials.

When I first met Bob, I thought, *How complicated can concrete be?* I soon learned that making concrete isn't as simple as stirring water into a bag of mixture and pouring. The composition changes based on proprietary blends and even intended uses.

He contracted and subcontracted with construction companies. One particular job tasked them with providing material for a training facility used by police and military personnel. Those facilities have a bullet ricochet problem because trainees use live ammunition. Bob frequented a shooting range and realized their concrete must have some special properties to absorb bullets. After all, the bullets can't bounce back and hit people, but they also can't punch through and contaminate the soil. So he studied the concrete used and developed his own concrete blend to keep trainees safe at the facility. The concrete he made would absorb the bullets, like a marble into Play-Doh.

Bob's concrete blend was a new invention. Together, we filed and secured a patent, and he used it on the training facility job. The happy client referred Bob to other firearms training grounds across the United States, where he also used the same patented formula. Soon word got around, and other construction companies and concrete contractors reached out. Bob's proprietary concrete blend became a valuable asset that could earn him revenue even when his company wasn't pouring concrete—those other businesses could license the formula.

Long story short, not all concrete is made equal.

That's IP.

Bob's bullet-absorbent concrete is an inventive solution to a real-world problem. Most patents are. I'll share another example.

I have a friend on the West Coast who's a serial entrepreneur and surfer. He buys businesses for a living and trains managers to run them so that he has time to enjoy surfing with his oldest son. They set out on a father-son adventure to ride the waves of the world outside California. That's when they encountered a problem—lugging around an enormous hard case to protect surfboards. They and other surfers they met were frustrated at having to load huge cases into tiny cars in developing countries.

Roy thought about the problem. His answer was a whole new case design. He and his son tried to create it themselves. They sketched up the blueprints but lacked the materials to build the case. So they contracted an engineer to design a prototype, then they contacted us to create a patent portfolio to protect it. Even though they couldn't manufacture the invention themselves, they explained the product in enough detail for someone else to build it. That's patent-worthy.

Of course, not all inventions are physical goods. I once worked with Raj, a serial software entrepreneur. One of his companies made safety systems. They put together old hardware components with new housings. Through that business, Raj also developed analytics software. Though lucrative, Raj's ideas were not focused on one commercial implementation.

I encouraged Raj to patent the software and its applications, in particular. He asked his investors, "Should I do this as one patent or break it up into six?"

"Six," they said. "More value!"

"But I'm just getting started," he told me. "Should I do this IP thing now?"

The answer to that question is usually yes. So that's what I told Raj.

As I got to work, we realized Raj needed a family of patents to cover the invention in all the ways he wanted to grow his company. So our firm secured a parent patent for Raj with children patents that allowed him to improve the software invention to incorporate updates and customer feedback. Eventually, we developed the parent patent into a family of over twenty patents. Based on those patents alone, he raised $15 million from investors. Patents are evidence of innovation. Investors love innovation.

Raj spun the analytics software into its own company. At scale, the business analyzed more content than any other public company globally. And when Raj was ready to move on to his next idea, he sold the company to a larger business.

That's right. IP assets can be sold, too. Those patents freed Raj to turn that company over to someone else without complication. And because he was selling a legally protected invention no competitor can recreate, Raj sold his business at a higher price than similarly sized software companies in his industry.

IP involving concrete, surfboard cases, and software may imply that an industrial or a technical background is the prerequisite for invention. They may—and they would be wrong.

I love clients who smash assumptions. There was a young lady named Taylor who had just graduated with an arts degree when she found Neo IP. As a teenager, Taylor self-taught design using open source software that provided online graphic art collaboration. The software's user base of over half a million had helped her improve over the years to become employable.

Then the creator decided to shut it all down. Adobe was discontinuing support for Flash, the software engine the site was built on. Taylor was devastated but undaunted. She reached out to the creator and offered a reasonable sum to buy the code. He accepted. Now what?

Taylor had a code but no coding skills. So I helped her explore a path forward. Even though Taylor did not know how the software worked like a coder, we talked about the program's features and functions—what it *could* be if it did everything Taylor wanted it to.

We then found a developer to design a wireframe for Taylor's new and improved art platform. We used that wireframe and her product road map developed with technical input to achieve the solutions she wanted to commercialize and filed a patent and a trademark application. Just like that, Taylor went from artist to tech founder—without being a tech person. Now Taylor has two assets—a patent and a trademark—combined with the existing platform and code that she can use to raise capital to grow the business.

IP assets can give you opportunities you never dreamed of while helping you foster the next generation of dreamers. Everyone wins.

Another young dreamer I had the pleasure of working with founded an event ticket resale app. Omar, like Taylor, was not a software developer. But his small, New York-based company was making money. Omar saw potential to scale if he could integrate social networking features to sign up more users. So he hired a software developer, explained the features he wanted, and had a platform built. When Omar and his developer demoed the app for me in the alpha phase, it was clear that he had something special. Together, we explored functionality, and we conducted the necessary patent research. Everything was on track for success.

Then the pandemic happened. In-person events and therefore ticket sales crashed. That didn't stop my client. We finished his patent paperwork during the lockdown so that he could relaunch his (patent pending) business when the world reopened. Omar's IP protected him even when his industry crashed. Because assets are leverage you don't lose, even if the business isn't active.

Another young client played in a band. Christopher came into my office talking about cryptocurrencies after he had started a business with a Bitcoin ATM. From there, Chris and another creative partner developed software for a music platform that could integrate cryptocurrency payments. We helped Chris secure patents to exclusive rights in the platform, and he built the business. Now he has the option of selling the business or licensing the patent portfolio and the platform he created. Everything combined with the IP assets has already multiplied the value of his business.

His future is brighter because he formalized the creation of his assets, not just operating the business. That's another observation I've made about IP over the years. Generally young people who create businesses are not encumbered by the assumption that patents, trademarks, copyrights, and the like are expensive or require excessively complicated prep work or time.

That's not to say all intellectual property is straightforward and intuitive. Some IP is complex because the inventions themselves are. One such example is the surgeon who encountered this problem: "I'm tired of closing surgical incisions manually or with staples that leave lifelong scars. I would like a high-tech suturing alternative." Typically, the more complicated the invention, the more a diverse team and skills are required. The surgeon collaborated with my former undergraduate professor and his colleague from another engineering business to develop that solution.

The two men observed the surgeon's hand movements and created a handheld device that recreated the precise motions for subcutaneous suturing. After developing a working prototype and engineering drawings, they contacted my firm to explore patentability. We researched the prior art and determined that, indeed, their invention was different from anything else in the patent system and on the market. We created a strategy to cover the device, the methods for using it, and the sutures created by it. They continued to evolve their invention and the corresponding patent applications. We secured granted patents for every aspect of their invention. Commercialization is another story. Often the inventors are not ultimately in a position to manufacture or sell their invention. So we connected them to companies who were active in that field, including contract manufacturers who could also assist them with the complications of regulatory approval. Fast-forward to today, and they have a family of patents and several generations of working prototypes.

Those intellectual assets opened up a whole world of business opportunities. The trio can raise capital for their own company, or they can license or sell their patents to a company that wants to improve medical care for everyone. There's no guarantee for success in patents, in business, or in life. But taking a calculated risk can help you make a positive impact by bringing your unique inventions into the world. All starting with ideas to solve problems and meet market needs.

Your assets can make the world better. And they can make your life better.

As long as you take the steps to transform your ideas into assets so that they can be deployed in a business.

Why Every Business Needs Intellectual Assets

None of the inventors you just met fall into the same category. Concrete formulations, software platforms for entertainment, and surgical devices have little in common. And yet all these creators, founders, and owners are poised to benefit from their intellectual property—whether they operate a business or transfer those assets to someone who does.

So what is intellectual property exactly, and how do you create it? IP is an intangible asset—an idea converted into transferable personal property rights through patents, trademarks, copyrights, service marks, and trade secrets. IP covers every famous animated character you've ever heard of, the logos on your clothing, and this book you're reading right now. IP covers products and services you use every day—from flashlights to mobile phones, packaging to cars, food and beverage products to smart thermostats. IP is not only for big businesses. Most start-ups and event microbusinesses have IP of some kind. So where do you look for it?

Intellectual property offers businesses incredible benefits. Because the value of business isn't just what the business does; it's also what the owner *knows*. The concrete business owner brought in concepts from a shooting range to create a new concrete blend. The artist had no idea how to create software, but she leveraged what she remembered of her own experience into a safe haven for other artists to learn and grow. And the surgeon didn't know how to solve the problem of automating the routine manual task of suturing; he just realized there was a problem that needed to be solved. But he did know what motions the device needed to replicate. That was the start of the IP process. Document what the problem is and what you imagine the solution to be, and then create it or collaborate with others to create it. If it works, and it's unlike anything else that exists, you may have what is required to create IP.

That's why it's called *intellectual* property. The creators, founders, professionals, investors, and owners thought up the idea. That idea belongs to them. And through law, that idea can be transformed as a valuable asset that can be used to create wealth—either by enjoying the exclusive rights to keep others out of your protected IP or by licensing or selling those exclusive rights to someone else who wants to do it.

Great ideas are useful for a business. Ideas are the one unlimited resource we have as human beings. Let's get real, though—ideas are free, and on their own are worth nothing. An idea—even a great idea—has no value. Except when the idea is transformed into some type of IP asset. Then it has real, tangible value, particularly if its exclusive rights cover a large, valuable market. The IP rights operate to exclude other companies and individuals from operating within your claimed territory. These IP rights in turn increase the valuation of a business because assets have a multiplying effect. A business without IP has no barriers to competition. A business with IP has exclusive rights that can make an existing business more valuable compared with its competition. A business with valuable IP may attract a larger company to acquire it, providing an exit and wealth event for the business owner and shareholders, if any. IP also attracts talent who want to be connected to innovation, impact, and growth; talented employees may contribute new ideas that further evolve or leverage your IP into something even better.

Consider the company that uses its patents to wow investors and buyers. They have a gallery in their headquarters that displays every patent they've ever received—and it's hundreds. They develop new ideas, patent them, prototype them, launch products, sell that business, and move on to the next one. When new companies visit to hear what they've done, they walk through the patent gallery and see how incredibly innovative the team is. That shows the quality of the ideas coming out of that company, and they want to collaborate with them or become part of that innovative team.

As I said earlier, IP is an indicator of innovation and provides a barrier to competition; if it's in a growth sector, then that combination attracts investors. And that allows for additional growth through new equity capital or growth financing that you might not otherwise acquire.

A tech founder who later became a client learned that the hard way.

"You don't need patents. You just need branding," my client's advisor told him. When that founder approached two investment funds, he heard something else.

"Why don't you have any patents?"

"How will you keep competition out of your market share?"

Filing a patent is a relatively small cost for the asset you're creating, and it multiplies the value of your current assets and the business overall.

Finally, creating IP is itself entrepreneurial. A patent can spawn a business in its own right, even without connections to operations, sales of products, or services. All seven of the clients I mentioned became founders through their IP, even if they were not entrepreneurs at the start of their inventive journey. Yet they left a lasting imprint on their industries and got their names in the history books for creating something new, unique, and uncopyable.

Every business needs IP. Whether it's patents, trademarks, copyrights, trade secrets, or even the contracts that you have with your employees, contractors, vendors, and customers. In fact, many owners and founders already have intellectual property, or at least the potential for it. Yet not everyone is aware that their most valuable business assets exist because they haven't considered everything that is IP—they haven't discovered or inventoried what creative solutions, competitive differentiation, or other business advantages exist in their companies already, or what they could create in the future.

Not Just for "Those Other Businesses"

When I speak to groups of business owners about IP, I get questions about global corporations and household name brands. The assumptions are many: IP is expensive, IP takes a big team, IP is for huge corporations. You file patents and sue people. If you can't afford to sue big companies, your IP isn't valuable. Some believe IP is like a lottery ticket: You file a patent and it's automatically worth millions. Maybe someone somewhere will pay you a million dollars for your idea, but it's not likely. Ideas on their own are not usually worth anything. Many companies stop there. Especially if you're small or early stage. I've lost track of how many times I've heard someone say, "IBM needs patents, but we're too small to do anything with patents."

Look at IBM's acquisition of Red Hat, Inc., which started small. Most people think Red Hat does not invest in patents because its business is based on open source software. It's actually the opposite: Red Hat has consistently invested in patents and enjoyed exclusive rights in its market. IBM benefitted from Red Hat's IP portfolio because they filled a gap in its own IP and services offerings. Without patents, Red Hat's valuation would have been much lower, and it's possible that the acquisition would not have even occurred.

All IP is about business. It's not just another asset class—it's often the greatest asset a company has, and we can't ignore it. Yet many people do just that until it's too late to file, such as after their invention is already in public use, or even years after product launch. Or they don't worry about IP at all, until they receive a cease and desist letter from a company that *did* file. Imagine being told you can't use your own idea anymore. How do you prove it was actually your idea? That's why you need to protect yourself.

Still, IP is more than law and lawsuits. IP is all about business assets. Intellectual property rights are intangible assets that provide exclusive rights to keep competition out of your market. And IP is all about solving problems in new ways. So if you're solving a problem in a unique way, then you may have an important business asset—intellectual property. And you may be able to sell that asset even *without* a company associated with it. When you have an idea, transform it into an invention, and file a patent, you are sowing a seed. Asset deployment is how you nurture it, what you grow it into. It's beyond filing a patent. It's building an intangible asset that may have value in the market. But you need to imagine how you're going to use it in the beginning—before you create this asset. Because the way you create the asset may determine its value and the limitations on how you use it or deploy it. It doesn't matter if you're an individual at a small or large company. Consider who it's valuable for and what it will do for them, and you can convert your ideas into capital to multiply your business—or to cash as a sale of the IP or business exit.

Unique Solutions, Tangible Assets

I'll say this again because it takes a few times to register with most businesspeople: Intellectual property is about solving problems. That means *your IP is your unique, invented solution* to a problem that affects you, your business, and others (hopefully a large market). It's helpful to think about it more as a business asset than as a legal issue or the law. The business asset is created by intellectual property legal activities, but it's the resulting asset that matters and how you will use it within your business or a market. Patents are inventive solutions to problems. Valuable patents are inventive solutions to real problems that people and companies care about for their markets. Most people who launch a business say, "I can do this better, and nobody has this take on it." *That* is inventing. So it's important to pay attention to what makes your business idea or operations different. What you do in your business may be an asset that you can legally protect. Much of it already is. For example, the copy on your website and your logo are both IP (hopefully you own the copyrights to these works; see chapter 6). Your operations manual is IP and may even include trade secrets. Your client base and customer service back end are IP. Even the service your business offers may have some IP associated with it. Legacy knowledge, documentation, how you hire, and your human resources systems include IP. Competitive intelligence is IP, too.

Every founder, owner, and leader operates their business differently. This differentiation is important to stay ahead of the competition. *How* you stay ahead—your unique solutions that no competitor has intuited yet—could have significant value for your business today and in the future.

This is true even if you don't yet imagine how it possibly could. In my experience, most people underappreciate how inventive their ideas are, particularly tech-savvy people. Especially software-based businesses. Software developers often create something and say, "Oh, this is nothing." But that code has value, particularly if its functionality or features are useful and different from existing alternatives. Meanwhile, other businesspeople say, "I'm not an inventor, so I don't need to file anything." But the overwhelming majority of patents—some suggest 98 percent or more—are improvements on existing inventions. If it's *your* unique improvement, it's *your* IP. And you deserve to own it. And profit from it.

Do yourself a favor: Read a few patents in your area. Identify five to ten problems in your business, market, or industry and then read patents about how other companies have solved them or tried to solve them. You'll be amazed by how simple this process is. You'll likely say to yourself, *Wow, I could have thought of that.* Some of you may have thought of that but didn't realize someone else was making money from the idea—or even could. The patent system is amazing— every patent is an inventive solution to a problem. And every patent is a teaching document—it describes the solution in a way that someone of ordinary skill in that area can make or use it. So it's like an instruction manual for how to solve the problem. If you can read, then you can teach yourself anything. And you can learn a lot about the evolution of solutions in any market or industry—just by reading patents.

Let's start with something simple. I helped a real estate business owner named Pam. She wanted wireframe FOR SALE signs to stick in the ground but found that existing signs didn't work well. Her real estate agents had a hard time shoving typical signs' stakes deep enough into hard ground, and usually they wouldn't stay upright in most weather conditions, especially in the wind. One day she realized that stabilization was important, so she invented a crossbar to attach to the sign frame she'd always used. The crossbar allowed agents to push the signs into the ground with only one foot without difficulty. And the positioning and construction of the crossbar was important for sign stability. That small but crucial improvement resulted in a patent. This type of IP exemplifies the opportunity for generating passive income through a license to other companies alongside her real estate business.

It's IP, yet it may not seem like important IP. Not at first. So here's a trick to help you identify factors that may lead to important IP assets. My favorite law firm mentor helped me imagine how useful features and functions are often the things to focus on for identifying valuable IP assets. This was his story: Consider the simple coffee mug. Someone, at some time, decided that a handle would be important. What makes it useful is that you can hold the hot mug by the handle without burning your hand. That question—"What makes this useful?"—is the heart of identifying potential IP. If other people or companies would find it useful, it is. And that is often what makes it valuable.

Two Important Questions to Ask Yourself about IP Right Now

Even if it's worth it, you might think looking into IP is going to be time-intensive, expensive, and stressful. And you can't even get started on your own, right? You don't know what you don't know, and what you do know may be wrong. For example, often people assume the IP process takes years, tens of thousands of dollars, and can be done only by a lawyer . . . or should never be done by a lawyer, and you should only do it yourself. Misconceptions abound.

I'll dispel most of the myths and mistakes in the first section of this book. Right now, let's talk about the two most important steps of the IP process, which we'll answer in the second section of this book. And these are a lot simpler than you might imagine.

1. "What Do I Have?"

Whatever you've invented, created, or thought up, document it. What's the problem you're solving, and how did you do it? You don't even need a prototype; you just need to explain it. Common law copyright boils down to this: "If you created it, it's yours." Trademarks begin the moment you start using it commercially, and trade secrets are protected, too.

The beginning of IP is capturing your solution in words and visuals so that you can communicate it to other people, including an IP lawyer. So make sure you write down your ideas. That's the best place to start, and it's a lot of the work. I wrote this book to show you how, step-by-step, with no part of the process skipped.

2. "Is It Legally Protectable?"

If it can't become intellectual property, it's not an asset. It's just an idea. A good lawyer can help you answer this question, but you'd be amazed by how easy it is to get legal protection for even an idea. As long as yours is a unique improvement on what already exists. Specifically, you'll be looking for a way to *transform* this information or knowledge into an asset you can *transfer*.

In this case, *transform* means leveraging your idea into a value based on who needs it. And *transfer* means anything from leveraging your idea to licensing it, from selling the idea to selling your whole business.

If your idea can solve a problem and can generate value, chances are excellent that you've got a legally protectable IP. Later in this book, I'll walk you through a simple checklist so that you know which of your ideas, processes, strategies, and tools have IP potential—and which don't.

The Number One Reason to Look into Your Intellectual Property

If it's not IP, it's not yours.

You feel ownership over your creation, your invention, your ideas. But if you don't legally claim them, you're donating them to the public—or to competitors. Say you've come up with a solution to a problem. Protecting that potentially valuable IP creates a limited monopoly to keep people out. It's like zone defense in basketball. IP rights help you own your zone—your competitive space where no one else can score. If the best offense is a great defense, then no offense is the worst.

In 1963, Robert Kearns invented intermittent windshield wipers. He marketed them to Ford, Chrysler, and General Motors, who all rejected his invention and then stole it for their own use. It took him ten years of legal battles to win damages, and he succeeded only because he'd patented his invention. Imagine if he hadn't.

The Jack Daniels whiskey company has always credited Reverend Daniel Call with instructing the company's founder on making their whiskey. But in 2016, the public learned that an enslaved African American, Nathan "Nearest" Green, was the true creator of the formula. Jack Daniels sells over thirteen million bottles per year these days. Imagine if the original creator and his family had received royalties on his IP.

The idea for Isaac Merritt Singer's famous sewing machine was actually stolen several times, first from the original inventor, John Fisher, and then from Elias Howe, the original thief. Howe patented his stolen idea and sued the second thief, Singer, for damages. The two ended up sharing profits while the original inventor, Fisher, got nothing.

Windshield wipers, whiskey, and sewing machines—don't let your idea be the next one stolen. And don't be the one who didn't act on the idea to create IP.

Protecting your IP is like buying a domain name. Once someone owns the address, no one else can have it. Unless they can buy it. There's no second place for domain names. And there's no second place for patents. Once you own a patent, you can exclude everyone else from using your claimed invention. If anyone tries to use it without your permission, you can sue them to enforce your exclusive rights and recover lost profits or reasonable royalty from the infringer. But if they patent the invention first, you're out of luck. It's a race to file—the first inventor to file wins. And there's no second place. So don't wait another day.

Ultimately, the cost of *not* looking into IP is losing everything. But IP is not about fear of missing out or losing everything. It's about creating assets that can multiply your business value. IP is a multiplier of a business value based on who can do what with it and how large the exclusive rights can extend. You can command a premium with IP. Otherwise you just have the value of your own metrics (profit-loss, EBITDA, etc.). IP position can be valuable—even more valuable the larger the business is. Think of it this way: Exclusive rights are valuable to a small operating company, but the larger the company, the more advantageous it is to enjoy those exclusive rights and keep competitors out of the market. That's why it can be useful in stimulating an exit—acquisition of IP assets (and the company that created them) gives a bigger company the opportunity to keep its large competitors out of the exclusive market covered by the IP. Since there's no second place, you have to buy it if you didn't build it. Consider Apple versus Samsung mega-litigation of smartphone patents; with hundreds of millions of dollars in quarterly profit at stake, Apple had great benefit from keeping competitors out of its market.

IP ownership is everything. You can't afford to ignore it. And you can't wait to do it later.

How This Book Will Help You Turn Your Ideas into Assets

I'm going to tell you what no other IP expert has revealed. Most intellectual property books are dry and hard to read. Most patents can be tedious to read as well. So I'll make this process easy to understand without bogging you down with unnecessary details. And I'll tell you entertaining stories to illustrate the points without getting into legal theory.

I wrote this book to bust myths, prevent mistakes, and show the way. I did *not* write it to be an IP law textbook or how to write your own patent or trademark applications. You might come up with a new idea while reading and wonder, *Can I get patents or trademarks for my business?* I don't know. But what if you can, and what if they're valuable assets? With this book, you'll begin to find out.

A quick reminder about how these chapters are laid out. As I said, the first section of this book covers what *not* to do. That includes shattering the myths around IP. The second section contains what to do and how to get started. I do not advise that you do it yourself (see chapter 3 for more details on the pitfalls of DIY).

Why debunk myths and prevent mistakes before learning? Because these myths and mistakes can be *fatal* to creating your intellectual assets. There are really only two areas at the beginning of a business that will ruin it. One is not having a securities lawyer (and making mistakes with securities issues). The other is IP—created too late or wrong. You get only one chance. You need to know how to do it right the first time.

Unfortunately, I've seen people and companies start on their IP too late. I've lost track of how many times I've heard, "If only I'd done this a month ago" or "This one mistake will stop me from doing everything I wanted to do."

In one case, the business owner waited until they had generated revenue from selling their first product. Two years later, they decided to try filing a patent application on the core invention. Too late. Inventors must file before public use, or you create a bar or block to patenting. You cannot wait until you have revenue to decide to file. You must consider the option before the products or services launch commercially. Outside the US, most countries require that you file the patent application before you have even published anything about it, or you create that same block. There's no way to fix this problem once you've created it.

In another case, the inventor had been working for years on a solution for a new cleaning composition. When we conducted prior art research to determine patentability, we found that someone else had filed earlier, and that issued patent not only prevented this inventor from getting a patent but also blocked their freedom to operate—so they couldn't even continue their business.

In yet another case, a young student pitched their invention at a business competition and won some money and recognition for their innovation. But they didn't explore filing a patent application until over one year later. Their pitch and public demonstration became a block to their ability to secure IP rights in the invention. Not knowing the rules doesn't fix the problem.

In another case, a software start-up raising funding for their new venture—all experienced professionals, engineers, and executives—launched their first version of the software before they pitched to investors. When asked about patents, they said they were working on them with an experienced patent attorney, so they were in the process of drafting patent applications with nothing filed or pending. But no one had asked how long they'd been selling their software. Until one investor did. After looking into it, they were almost exactly at the one year mark when they would have been barred from patenting (or future patents would likely be invalidated by this public use or publication, making them worthless). Needless to say, they were in a rush situation to complete the filings before the anniversary of the sale.

Hearing these sad cases over and over is heart-wrenching. But you cannot turn back the clock and fix these problems. Many entrepreneurs fail to protect their ideas and lose their chance. Don't let it be you. Explore IP before it's too late.

As we go through this book together, keep in mind that IP is not just for companies that want investors. It's also for companies whose owners want to sell (eventually) or continue operating. One of my clients came in after receiving a cease and desist letter about their company name. They'd been using it since day one, but another company adopted a similar name afterward and then sued to protect what they thought was their own IP. This client could have won the litigation but would have lost $150,000 or more in legal costs because they didn't invest in securing their own IP. The litigation would have destroyed their business. It's another example of why you have to explore investing in IP sooner, not later.

The good news is that we helped them navigate the problem to avoid the litigation process, resolve the dispute, and save their business. I'll teach you some of those methods in this book.

Don't wait until it's too late. Learn about IP, secure your assets, protect yourself, and discover the value that your IP assets have—they can multiply your business value. That's what this book will do for you. Let's start by setting straight some of the most common IP misconceptions.

SECTION 1

IP MYTHS AND MISTAKES

CHAPTER 2

IP MISTAKE: FAILING TO DEVELOP AN IP STRATEGY

Imagine you want to become the world's best video editor. You-Tubers need support, and you want to work with the stars. You're headed for fame and fortune!

The only problem is, you need a new computer. You go to the store and walk down the computer aisle. But they all look the same. You don't know which one to choose. So you buy one at random.

What are the odds that a random computer meets your exact needs? Pretty low, right? Video editing takes up a lot of processing power. And you're probably going to want a top-of-the-line graphics card. You might even want a removable graphics card instead of an internal one so that you can upgrade the card as better hardware becomes available. You also want to pick a reliable brand that won't crash on you and destroy your hard work.

You don't just "buy a computer." If you don't check the computer's specs, you won't know if the one you're buying will meet your needs. You have to know what it can do before you buy it.

Buying a computer at random makes no sense. Yet this is how most people approach getting patents. It goes about as wrong as you can imagine.

People believe a lot of myths about IP. These myths result in mistakes, many of which cannot be undone or corrected. I've seen misfiled patents collapse entire companies. Imagine your life's work gone in a moment because you did not file properly. It happens more often than you think. Since you're reading this book, it likely won't happen to you. You know how valuable a successful filing can be . . . and how a failed one isn't. It's worth less than free.

You deserve better. IP is not just an idea; it's an intangible asset that does a specific job for you. Each one is different—patents, trademarks, copyrights. The specific way you get that job done is what you're protecting, and the way you do it affects the asset value.

How Do I Actually File a Patent?

Your filing process will vary depending on what type of IP you have. You might ask, "Can't I just fill out this patent form I found online?"

I heard about an entrepreneur who was very experienced in the biomedical industry. He hired an attorney to file a patent application. But the lawyer didn't think to ask him, "Is this idea even patentable?" The entrepreneur didn't think to ask either. That mistake cost the client a fortune in unnecessary legal fees and a useless, expensive patent. Getting a lawyer on your side may not help you if that lawyer isn't experienced in patents.

Every IP is unique and needs to be approached as such. First, document what it is and how it works. You must be able to explain your IP—in layman's terms—in such exacting detail that someone could reproduce it from the patent alone. Leave out a step, and it's not a patent. You can include any graphics and drawings necessary. Know exactly what you plan to claim, because those claims are your value. The claims of a patent are the business and legal value of the patent. The claims mark the territory that is exclusively yours—often referred to as the metes and bounds of your invention, like a survey of real estate property to mark the property line. You can build a fence to keep others out of your property, but you can only build the fence on your property, not outside of those lines. Patent claims define your exclusive property rights, not the entire description of the patent. So it's important to understand what your claims cover and how they relate to the products and services your business offers.

Once you've compiled all this documentation, your lawyer drafts a patent application and files it. Congratulations! You're patent pending. But then you wait in the backlog. Waiting takes a long time, usually between eighteen to twenty-four months and sometimes much longer, depending on the volume of patent applications filed before you in that space. There are mechanisms that can help you move forward faster and even jump the queue. But if you don't know to ask about them, you might not be told about them (remember that most lawyers are reactive, not proactive, and so respond to what you ask them to do for you). One mechanism that we like to call fast-track or expedited examination allows you to pay an additional fee to get to the front of the line—for example, if you have an invention that addresses specific issues like COVID-19 during the early stages of the global pandemic in 2020 or energy efficiency that addresses environmental issues. Also, if you're over sixty-five years old, you can file a petition to make your application "special" to speed up your process. One client of another attorney I know learned about that special petition too late. He could have petitioned to be at the front of the line but didn't know to ask about it. He had been waiting for his patent for ten years, and it still had not been granted.

In my experience, many patent attorneys don't typically advise people about these options. They assume you don't want to pay more money to expedite the process or inquire about age or special inventions for which you could file a petition to be at the front of the line. Again, most attorneys are reactive, not proactive. So it's helpful to know what your options are before you hire an attorney, or at least ask about timing, options to expedite, special options, and so forth.

Maybe your needs are specific. You may not want to expedite your patent application because the development and commercialization will take longer than in other industries (e.g., in pharmaceuticals or other regulated markets). You may not want your patent application to be published until it's issued, to remain in stealth mode and prevent competitors from reading your application before you have enforceable rights (only granted patents are enforceable; patent pending is more like a KEEP OFF THE GRASS sign than a fence to keep others out of your exclusive property). You can file a nonpublication request at the time you file your application if you don't plan to file internationally. But you must make that choice at the time of filing—you cannot do it later during prosecution. It is my hope that this book will help you become more aware of the options you have so that you can plan a strategy instead of merely filing in the most basic way.

Sometimes you want your patent published as fast as possible. The primary reason for that choice is to put competitors on notice, labeling your invention "patent pending." That's like a bold statement that says, "Back off. I expect to have exclusive rights in this claimed area, and this is your notice to avoid infringement when my patent issues." Remember that the patent system is based on an exchange of publishing the inventive solution for rights to exclude others for a limited time—the twenty years of life of the patent. So generally, publishing eventually becomes part of the process.

The point is, you have ways to control the speed of publishing. Depending on your situation, one choice may be disastrous while another is perfect. If you do this alone or with an attorney who isn't proactive in helping you, you could be left in a difficult or bad situation.

This is why it's important to build your patent strategy *before* you begin the filing process. Start with the why. This is true for patents, trademarks, and service marks. Why do you want to secure IP rights in this idea, invention, or brand? What do you want the IP to do for you in your business? How will you use the IP? Will you operate your business and make/use/sell the products or services covered by IP? Or do you intend to try to license or sell the IP to someone else?

You may file a trademark as "intent to use" to ensure that you have the earliest possible priority date for your trademark. Or you might have been using the mark with goods or services in commerce already and need to file on another basis. You might choose to combine different types of use (classes of goods or services) in a single filing. Or you might want to file separate marks instead of writing all the descriptions of goods and services together. For example, if I'm going to launch a security surveillance company, I may have a SaaS platform (service) and equipment (goods). We typically advise separating these applications because in the future my business may continue providing one class of goods or services but not another. Trademarks can last indefinitely as long as there is continued use and the registrations are maintained.

Even the research is crucial. If you find that someone else has a prior pending mark on a similar IP, the way you write the goods and services sections to differentiate your IP from that other mark may determine whether you will be accepted or rejected. If you don't study the competition, you may file for something that isn't likely to result in a registration. That means you wasted time and money.

The same goes for patents. Researching the prior art is optional; there is no requirement to do it before you file a patent application. Some attorneys advise that you don't want to do this research at all, because it is the US Patent and Trademark Office (USPTO) examiner's job to do this research. (Some people advise that you don't want to know what's patented so that you won't risk being accused of willfully infringing on someone else's patent. But you're deemed to know about it anyway, because it's published. And there's no better time to design around someone else's claimed invention than when you're developing the product or service; it saves time and money and is evidence of a good faith effort to avoid infringement.) If you wait until the examiner conducts the prior art research (months or years after the application is pending), you may find that you are not likely to be successful in getting the patent to issue. Wouldn't you rather know in advance what your chances are?

Although it's not a requirement, I advise all clients to have patentability research and analysis conducted as a first step for these reasons: (1) you have an early indication of likelihood of success for patenting; (2) you can differentiate from the prior art identified and include that content in your patent application, thereby making it more likely that you will be successful in the prosecution with the patent examiner; and (3) you can identify other alternatives that you may wish to explore within your own patent application. Most inventions are new combinations of known components. You can invent only from what you know. The more patent data you see, the more you know about how solutions have evolved over time in any scientific or technological field. Finally, patent data from this research and analysis of the relevant context of your invention can inform your patent strategy (how you file applications) and your business strategy. Patent data is a leading indicator of market activity. It is a rich source of information about competitive activity as well.

You need a strategy. Fortunately for you, I've developed one.

How I Developed My Own IP Strategy: The Patent Forecast Story

My company developed software with exceptional functionality, both on the back end and on the front end with visualization—we applied evolutionary biology principles as algorithms to patent data so that we could literally see how science and technology solutions were evolving as evidenced by the patent system. We wanted the exclusive rights to our solution for the specific features we designed and invented.

We could have just filed a patent saying, "Here's how our software functions." For example, our software featured a dynamic timeline that no competing software had. Yet we continued thinking beyond one aspect of the software. We also had context data, categories of technology, different categories that listed who owned what, and a host of other unique features. We also thought about alternatives for user interface interactivity. When we explored the prior art, we realized that our dynamic, interactive visualization with updateable timeline was truly differentiated, but it was also our valuable, *exclusive* feature that made us distinctive and relevant in the market.

Even before we built all the features we imagined, we were already expanding on the product and process. We explored our future feature sets as a product road map and filed patent applications covering what we were creating and what we planned to create in the future. So this is an example of how to go beyond what you are launching immediately when you create your patent strategy and execute it. Instead of just building a fence to protect your immediate territory, plan how to put more territory within your fence and extend your boundaries now. Just like your business is not static, the patent process is not static. So your patent strategy needs to be informed by data continuously.

It's dynamic like weather forecasting—that's one reason we use our own Patent Forecast software to explore the current patent context, and we continue to watch it as it changes every week when new patents are issued and new patent application publications are made by the USPTO.

As I just mentioned, to clearly differentiate our invention from similar ideas, we did patent research and competitive research. Patent examiners are always looking for the reasons to reject you, because it's their job to ensure that only valid patents are issued. With this in mind, we had to write our patent applications to avoid those potential objections or rejections. By anticipating what will happen during prosecution with the patent examiner, we create more robust applications when we differentiate from the start. Absolutely distinguishing our idea from everyone else's improved the likelihood of success with our filing. Even better, it streamlined the prosecution so that we had fewer exchanges with the patent examiner. This saved time and money overall.

Software is always improving and always upgrading. So our patent strategy included plans for additional child patents claiming priority to our initial filing so that we could expand our patent families whenever we had a new important feature or function.

We also wanted trademarks to protect our goods and services as part of our overall IP strategy. The simplest way to think about a trademark is a word, mark, or symbol that says, "Only products or services with this mark are authentically from us, and only *we* can sell it."

We secured a trademark for Patent Matrix. We also secured a trademark registration for Patent Forecast for our software offering.

We registered these specific trademarks because we knew they would be valuable and distinctive from other competitors who wanted two-word combinations: "Patent + Word." If they want to operate in that space with similar services or products, they have to work with us. We knew our name had to be distinctive to our offerings yet also attractive to the largest companies if we decide to sell our business in the future.

Imagine doing all this from scratch with no idea how the IP process works or what your future might look like. Without a plan for creating and maintaining IP assets while your business grows and changes, you may block yourself. And you can't fix it later. Without a strategy, companies may file too many patents, not only in the US but also internationally, which is very expensive and may not be likely to return value for that investment. Some companies get choked into bankruptcy because of poor patent strategy or no strategy.

Doing it right doesn't just protect you from disaster. It also helps make you prosperous and more attractive to partners or potential acquisition-minded companies.

If I want to raise investment capital or funding to grow and scale my business, I can use patents and patent pending assets to support a higher valuation. Since I have a limited monopoly to exclude others with clear lines, there is a barrier to competitors for my target market, so the investment is derisked from that perspective. If I decide to sell, the patent multiplies the value of the revenue, profit, and everything else associated with the business.

A larger company benefits more from IP exclusivity because they have greater distribution with more marketing and more salespeople. But patents give my software company power. If a competitor—whether a large company or a small company—infringes on my patent, I can use IP assets to enforce my exclusive rights.

Generally, most companies don't intend to infringe. Companies that own patents respect other companies that have patents. But be advised that most companies do not conduct clearance research to ensure that they are not infringing; large companies may operate in areas that are exclusive to others' IP rights. Why? Because there are no patent police. You have to be prepared to enforce by maintaining access to early priority dates in your original patent applications; you have to continue expanding and modifying claims and keep this "continuation practice" as a reasonable way to ensure that you can revise claims to target anyone who enters your exclusive space. Filing child patents as continuations or continuation-in-part applications keeps this option open.

If you approach your IP incorrectly, or without a strategy, you not only will lose time and money but also may forfeit the opportunity to secure the IP. You may block yourself. Or allow competition to block you. There is no second place. If you get rejected and don't have a quality application, you may have to start over from scratch or fail to secure the IP entirely. Now you're years behind somebody else in line or blocked completely. Someone else might have filed in between your first submission and your second and may beat you to the finish line.

Imagine losing your patent, trademark, or other IP rights because you didn't have a strategy that is aligned with your business or that anticipates changes in the market, the technology or science, or the competition's activity. That's heartbreaking. Don't cheat yourself. Have a plan in place before you start.

The Four-Step Prefiling Checklist

Before I even begin to file, I take four nonnegotiable steps. Skipping even one could be catastrophic. But if you follow all four steps, your filing process will be targeted toward your exact needs.

1. Know How to Use It

As you consider getting patents, the first question to ask yourself each time is, "What do I want this patent to do for me?" A patent for running a business and a patent for licensing are different animals. If someone can easily design around your license, a patent is unlikely to protect you.

You use your own IP, so you know it. But you need to make sure you *really* know it, backward and forward. You also need to know how you want to use it in the future.

We knew for sure we would use our Patent Forecast software as a company and enjoy the exclusive rights secured by our IP. We also wanted to have the option to license it, if we identified key partners or strategic collaborators. Though we had no plans to sell the assets instead of operating the business, the IP assets have value on their own as well as coupled with the software and business; we could sell it someday if we want to.

You must consider at the outset whether you want to license your IP. If you do, you need to understand how your licensees will use it. Your IP assets must be strategically developed for licensing—if it's easy to design around your patents, no one will need to license from you. So you'll need to consider alternatives to your preferred inventive solution and include content to block others from designing around your claims. Protect that aspect, too.

In one example, the company developed a new security system that went beyond surveillance—they invented a solution to deter theft of delivered packages. Their initial description was focused only on the precise design. When we explored their business strategy, it became clear that their IP could be expanded to cover alternatives that would extend beyond that precise design. By broadening the scope of the described invention, their patents would have more value to their current business and ensure value for potential licensees or even stim-ulate interest from larger companies for acquisition of the IP assets.

2. Document It

You know how you want to use it, but what *is* your invention? Do you know what you have? You need to describe it to such an extent that anyone picking up your patent could understand at a glance what your IP is and what it does.

We had to ask, "What is Patent Forecast software now? What could it be? Where are we going with it?" We wanted our patent filing description to anticipate as many scenarios, features, and functionality as possible. So we documented everything, starting with what we had designed and developed before public use or publication, followed by what we might build in the future according to our product road map.

Part two of the description writing process focuses on the competition. How might someone else try to work around it?

Think beyond what you've created. What similar features could someone else develop? Instead of considering only our most preferred radian visual, we imagined alternative visualizations, interactive user interfaces, and data sources. For example, we considered that our software could apply to technology descriptions and market data, not just patents and patent data.

While you're describing your IP for this documentation step, think about how someone else might see it. What possibilities change when you step out of your creator box and view it as a competitor or as a user? Are there other applications or modifications that might make it better? You need as many perspectives on your invention as you can get. And you need to build those perspectives into your documentation.

3. Research Existing Patents

Patent examiners usually reject patent applications, at least initially. I was a patent examiner before I became a patent attorney, so I understand that the role of a patent examiner is to challenge the application claims to ensure that only valid patents are issued.

You need to think like an examiner. Know why you might be rejected before you file. Is this invention even patentable? Is it possible to register this trademark? Raw data is necessary to answer these questions. Most of the time, the answer is yes, you can patent it or register the trademark, but only if you differentiate it from existing patents and trademarks in key ways. You can't begin this critical step of differentiation if you haven't conducted the research and analyzed what has existed previously.

Let's focus on patents here. Most patents are improvements—that is, they are new combinations of known components. It's rare to have truly revolutionary inventions in any sector. So let's explore how much improvement is needed to be patentable. For example, your improved widget may have five important features. The patent examiner conducts research and finds two prior patent documents—one that has two features of your widget and another that includes the other three features. The examiner will combine these prior art documents to reject your five claimed features, and that combination is the basis for rejecting your patent application. All you can do at that point is argue and lose, if you haven't anticipated that the examiner would do this. You need to do your homework, researching prior art to identify what an examiner might use to reject your claims, and build differentiation into your description and into your patent application. This proactive positioning streamlines your patent prosecution and improves your likelihood of success in obtaining a patent.

If a patent cost between $10,000 and $15,000 to file, wouldn't you want to know beforehand if it was going to succeed? I bet you're thinking, *Of course! Who wants to waste $10,000?*

And you're right! That's like throwing money into the air and hoping it lands in your pocket. Nobody in any industry *doesn't* want to do research when money is on the line. It's so critical that, in a later chapter, I'll give you a step-by-step preparation process to counter competitors.

For now, we're focusing on what *not* to do with patents, trademarks, and copyrights because the cost of mistakes is so high. We helped a new client who started the process with another law firm— they had been rejected eight times over twelve years. Another client spent ten years arguing against the patent office through a different firm and never achieved success. When we picked up their cases, we noticed that neither the previous law firms nor the clients had conducted prior art research and made differentiation a part of their patent application. So they spent years and tens of thousands of dollars trying to get anything they could, to no avail. You can't turn back the clock to correct this type of situation. There are possibilities to try to move forward, but the loss of time and money is impossible to fix.

Here's the bad news: Most law firms don't do patent research. Why? Because it's not a requirement for filing a patent application. They don't ask, and you don't know to ask for it. You may not know how it would help you. A search may turn up inventors who never commercialized their inventions and identify companies you didn't know filed before you. You need to know about the prior art publications and prepare to overcome rejections that a patent examiner might make initially.

Because this step is critical to successful IP asset creation— whether you are a start-up or a decades-old corporation—we'll be returning to patent research in the next chapter.

4. Secure Ownership

Who created your IP? Who owns it?

This is often a problem with early business ventures, start-ups, and young entrepreneurs. It's not uncommon for business or entrepreneurship students to collaborate on a new business idea and make a prototype, but they have not created a company or have an operating agreement among themselves. The result of the class project may include patentable inventions, copyrightable website content, and a cool brand. But not everyone wants to continue working on the project or invest, so who owns the IP (or potential future IP)? Can the people who want to continue launch a company with exclusive rights? What about the other team members who cocreated the IP?

Consider this example. Four students come up with an idea that solves an important problem and decide to work together to develop it into a business. They might even win some money in a pitch competition. Without legal agreements, everyone owns what they create—not four shares of 25 percent ownership; four people with 100 percent ownership of whatever they create or invent. So what happens if only two of the four students want to form a company (like a limited liability company) to continue to advance their invention? The two others get job offers and no longer want to work on it. Each of the four students needs to legally assign their invention and receive something in return for assigning it. Otherwise, the latter two could decide to sell their ownership or license to someone else. And the company is crippled from raising capital because they don't wholly own the IP.

Start-ups can have several cofounders. You need to think through what happens when somebody quits and leaves the early stage company. Who created the IP, and who owns it? Those are two different questions that have equally important answers.

Consider an example of an early stage company that is started with two founders. One is technically skilled and develops the software that the company will sell; the other is the CEO business development and sales lead. They raise preseed or seed investment capital from friends and family, where no one asks the standard diligence questions about IP ownership. The cofounders spend the funds to develop and launch the software after they file their first patent and trademark applications. The trademark application is filed in the company name.

The patent application is filed in the inventor names without being assigned to the company. Later, the overextended, weary CEO decides to leave the company to pursue a job elsewhere; that cofounder may still own some stock in the company or have partnership stakes. Without an assignment document to confirm that the company owns the IP, that cofounder still co-owns the patent application (and future patent). The friends and family investors and the remaining cofounder are left without wholly owning the IP that they expected. The former CEO could license or even compete directly with this business because of co-ownership of the patent assets. Imagine the challenge of trying to get an assignment document executed after the cofounder has left (maybe even because of disagreement or not on good terms).

It's critically important that any company have agreements—contracts—in place for every person, even the founders to assign any and all rights they have in the IP. Before any significant progress is made, ensure that everyone agrees to assign the ownership to the company.

Make ownership decisions and execute agreements before your idea becomes valuable and before partnerships end or cocreators leave the group or company.

Many companies don't have assignment of rights or confidentiality and nondisclosure agreements with their contractors and employees. That's operating in dangerous waters because they could lose their IP position at any time and possibly cripple their business.

Consider another example. A company hired a software development group for custom software development based on ideas that the company held as confidential and proprietary. The first company paid the dev group $500,000 for the custom software, with a confidentiality agreement but without an IP assignment agreement. Because software code is content covered by copyrights, whoever writes the program owns the copyrights. That means the company just paid a fortune for software they don't even own—they have only a license to the deliverable.

Sounds crazy, right? We encountered a similar problem with a client who contracted a software development group to create custom software along those fact lines. There was a confidentiality agreement but no assignment or work-for-hire agreement. The software deliverable worked well for their complicated testing and data analysis, so they were happy. Until they discovered that the software dev group was offering the same software to our client's competitors. We had not been asked to review the software dev contract; the corporate attorney did not think about IP rights and assignment, so they weren't addressed. Thankfully, we leveraged the confidentiality clause that was included in the development agreement. It provided that the software dev group could not disclose to any third parties the confidential material our client provided to them, which was an essential part of the software deliverable. So the company was able to block the sale to competitors, but they still didn't have the ownership rights that they thought they were buying when they contracted for the work.

Without a work-for-hire and assignment of rights agreement, the first company owns nothing except a license to use the deliverable. If they want improvements, they cannot simply take the software to another developer. They have to go back to the original company because of the copyright ownership. If you have not obtained assignment of ownership from anyone, all you own is a license in the case of copyrights. In the case of other IP, you might own nothing.

Even your contracts are assets. Vendors and employees also affect your intellectual property. You need to know if you own your IP or if your contractors or vendors do. Can your vendors sell to competitors? Maybe they can. You may be able to address it now with the right contract. Don't wait until it's too late.

Is there any value to exclusivity? Is this relationship an asset? If so, you want a contract that documents it. You also need to look into confidentiality, noncircumvent, and nonuse clauses in agreements. In today's social media and digital world, it's also important to consider nondisparagement clauses to protect your brand and reputation in addition to owning the IP.

Ownership involves planning—you have to contract before the IP is created to avoid many problems, like those illustrated in this chapter. You don't want to write yourself out of the game by stumbling into these dangerous but invisible traps. Like patentability research, patent ownership is either a green light or a stop sign on the journey to building an IP asset. You can correct the ownership later, but it may be difficult, costly, and even painful. So we'll be revisiting ownership in depth in an upcoming chapter.

To DIY or Not to DIY?

You might read this chapter and think, *OK, sure, I've got the checklist. The patent office has an FAQ and forms. I need an abstract, some figures, and a description of claims. I'll write mine mimicking a template. Good enough.*

These are the *minimum* requirements. Following them will get you an application that meets the minimum requirements. It does not mean that you have created a valuable asset.

If you follow the minimum requirements, you will get rejected, most likely. You will argue with the patent examiner and fail. Then you'll pay a patent attorney a fortune for help and get rejected again because your lawyer only had your applications meet minimum standards to just get the job done. Even if you can get a patent granted, the claims may be so narrow that it is easy to design around them. That means your patent is not valuable because your exclusive rights are not broad enough to have commercial importance.

You'll be out both time *and* money. And someone else might improve on your minimum filing in the meantime and block you from using the improved, valuable solution because they have secured IP rights in it. So meeting the *minimum* requirements to file a patent is *not* the way to secure a patent asset that will be worth the time, energy, and money you invest. And it is *not* the way to create IP assets that multiply the value of your business. In the next chapter, you'll see why.

CHAPTER 3

IP MISTAKE: DIY (DO-IT-YOURSELF) FILING

I will always remember the sign I read in a dry cleaner's front lobby: Dry Cleaning Is NOT a Do-It-Yourself Project. I laughed when I read it. Then I thought about it and realized, *Holy smokes, they're right!* The company deployed that sign when home dry cleaning kits first hit the market. Suddenly everyone had the choice to DIY dry cleaning at home. But just because you can doesn't mean you will get the results you desire.

You don't dry clean your T-shirts and jeans. You reserve that effort for your best clothes—the garments you wouldn't want to accidentally destroy. I priced my best suits and dresses, compared that number to the cost of having a professional do my dry cleaning, and decided I would never attempt it myself. The consequences were just too high, even if the risk might have been relatively low.

Just because you *can* DIY dry clean doesn't mean you should—or that it will turn out well. The same is true of DIY patents. But the risk is much higher, and the consequences are higher still. You can replace your best suit, but you can't replace the best idea you've ever had. If you're trying to save money by writing your own patent application, you're risking what may be the most important asset in your business. You're gambling with stakes you can't afford to lose.

I'm going to tell you a DIY patent horror story. An independent inventor decided to file his own provisional patent application, following the minimum requirements listed on the USPTO website. He raised money from investors to launch the business and continue the patent filing process. He filed a nonprovisional patent application claiming priority to the provisional filing, within the one-year period described on the patent office website. He met the minimum requirements. After another two years, he received the first office action wherein the patent examiner rejected the application—not only the claims but also the description or specification of the application. It was only three pages of content. Meanwhile, he launched his product on the market and had public use. When he brought the patent situation to our firm, we had to deliver the bad news. The DIY application was inadequate to create a valuable patent at that point because it would require a lot of new content to fully enable the description and support the claims he needed. Adding new material was possible, but he created a block for himself when he launched his product commercially. It was too late to correct. He was unable to get a patent on his product. By relying on his low-quality, DIY patent application, he made a huge mistake that was not possible to fix. Eventually the business ceased operations after it lost what could have been exclusive rights for that product in the market.

Here's another DIY horror story—a DIY contract that put an entire company out of business. The CEO of a technology company thought he could write a licensing contract for the company's key assets: its patents. Licensing is one way to monetize your IP, so the strategy may have been great, but the execution was tragic. Since the company couldn't develop every market sector while deploying their patented solution, licensing to other companies in these markets under a field of use is a reasonable option. He downloaded a template for the contract online and filled it out on his own.

With a patent portfolio license like that, licensors will typically grant a particular patent to the licensee for a particular use or for a limited field of use. It specifically defines what licensees are allowed to do with the patented technology, in what applications, markets, and geographies, and for what period of time. If they want to do more, they need to pay more.

Instead of saying, "You have exclusive license to *only* these things," the CEO chose a template contract that said, "You get exclusive license to everything *except* what's in this list."

Except he left the list blank. So his DIY contract licensed everything to a single licensee—and even blocked the company from acting on its own, in its existing markets.

Think about that for a moment. The CEO gave away the rights to use the patented technology to that licensee for all applications and all uses. He essentially eliminated his entire business for the payment from that DIY contract! As a result, his company was no longer able to operate. And when they tried to negotiate with the other company to reconsider that signed contract, what do you think they said? "Sorry, the contract says we have to agree in writing to amend it, which we don't. Why would we? We got an incredible deal." It wasn't nice or fair, but it was all because of the DIY contract problem.

Investors had put millions of dollars into this company, and now they had no chance to get a meaningful return on their investment. Employees lost their jobs. The nightmare continued for months—the error, the catch, the attempted fix, the refusal, and the brick wall.

The worst part was that the CEO had several law firms that represented the company. He should have known better than to DIY, and he didn't hire any of the outside law firms to check his work. He assumed that he could do everything himself, which would save the legal fees, and that it would all turn out fine. Until it didn't. Then the law firms were engaged and thousands of dollars were spent trying to correct the situation, unsuccessfully.

When we aren't sure what we're doing, we usually take our time at first. Then we get frustrated, shrug, and scribble down what we think is the right answer. At least it's done. If something isn't perfect, we'll just fix it later. What's the worst that could happen?

In this case, the worst outcome did happen. That CEO lost everything, including the patent assets that were the foundation of the business, and had to explain to everyone involved how he destroyed their investments and their jobs with one DIY contract.

Gambling with Others' Money

I'm not telling you to hire a professional so you'll hire me. I don't even do my own contracts and securities work because I remember that CEO horror story. I *could* do my own corporate work, but I refuse. I hired a law firm. It's too important for me to risk missing an important line and losing everything.

If I, an IP professional, hire my own lawyer to do the work for me, anyone who isn't an IP professional is well advised to do the same. It's that important to cover your bases and protect yourself. You have no reason to gamble with something you can't afford to lose.

Here's the first principle: If you're going to take other people's money at some point, get a lawyer. Even if you don't lose everything, you may still waste your time and money without one. And your patent may prove worthless when you need protection. The majority of patents are not commercially viable because they are not strategically filed.

If you're filing a patent to protect yourself, but you don't know how to file the patent so that it protects you, why are you filing at all? And if you're afraid of someone stealing your idea, why wouldn't you spend the money to keep it safe? It's like worrying someone will break in your front door and duct taping it shut. Duct tape cannot replace a deadbolt.

Even starting the IP filing yourself is not a good idea. A lawyer friend of mine says that every time a new IP client comes in and states, "I wrote and filed this myself," the law firm has to charge double just to undo what's already been done.

And a word to the wise: Being a good writer doesn't mean you can write a patent. It's not just a document; it's an asset. Plenty of good writers hire me to fix their mistakes, often when their patents or trademarks have been rejected. Responding to a rejection isn't usually enough. We often have to start over, which costs a lot of extra time and money.

Legal fill-in-the-blank websites give you fields to complete that meet the minimum requirements to file. The minimum is not an asset. You won't learn about most of the loopholes until you've missed out. On the DIY path, you don't know what you don't know until it's too late.

Remember in school when the teacher gave your book reports length requirements? The USPTO doesn't do that. Most DIY filers write three or four pages, when most patents should have descriptions between twenty and fifty pages long. You may think doing 10 percent of the work is good enough, then just like in school, you get it back stamped with an F. Only this time, that bad grade costs you thousands of dollars. One student inventor followed the minimum requirements for a patent application on the USPTO website, so he had patent pending status. He asked me to review it and give feedback—after he filed. The problem was that the description was only one page of solid content. So the application was worthless. He had wasted his time, and the government filing fees, and had to start over.

Even trademark applications can suffer under DIY. One of my new clients had filed their own trademark application and received a rejection because the description was too close to an already registered trademark. They didn't research before they filed; they didn't differentiate. They had to start over and reconsider the description; we helped them craft an accurate description of their services while also differentiating over the existing prior registration that actually covered another area. Do-overs always cost more—*if* you even can try again. Trademarks are more forgiving than patents in this respect, unless someone else has filed before you get it right. Remember, there is no second place in IP—you have to get there *properly*, and you have to get there first.

Most people don't know what they don't know. For example, public use blocks your invention from valid patenting. A DIY filing that is inadequate gives a false sense of security; if you DIY file improperly and then proceed with your business activity and commercialization, you actually bar your own properly created IP. You become your own obstacle without ever knowing it. The meetings I have with people where I have to explain how they ruined their own chances to patent are full of anguish and sometimes even tears. I don't want anyone to be in that position.

"I'll file later after I make money," I hear from creative, high tech software entrepreneurs. Once it's being used publicly, that's too late. You have to file before you even talk about it or publish it, if you have interest in international patenting. There is a grace period for publication in the US, and public demonstration may fall within that grace period—for example, introducing products or services on your website, appearing at a trade show, entering a pitch competition, and other uses. This is considered a publication, so you have to file within one year. But once you start selling commercially and have public use, it's too late for a patent application. And it's first to be accepted or nothing. Even if you file for a patent *before* publishing, if the patent application is incomplete, or someone else has filed before you did, the patent examiner will reject your application. Then you'll go back and forth, back and forth, arguing. Or you'll have to start over from scratch and refile a better, more complete application, one that is differentiated from the prior art. But what if another company has filed a similar patent? You're behind them in the queue now. So they may claim "your" intellectual property territory first. IP is worth doing right the first time because there is no silver medal. There is no second place for patents.

So I say to you what I practice myself and tell my loved ones: Don't DIY patents or trademarks. You'd be better off lighting the application fees on fire—at least you'd have some entertainment for a short time.

A friend once showed me his draft patent application for a consumer product. He used a cheap online service to put it together. No prior art research. And his draft filing didn't meet the minimum for acceptance, so I told him he hadn't written enough to support the business and legal value of his claims. He was crushed, but I saved him the worse heartache of being rejected, losing his money, and risking someone blocking him by properly patenting over the thin core of invention that his publication disclosed. He's now gone back to development to create the differentiation needed in the crowded consumer product space of his invention.

The Only Two Instances DIY Does Apply

First, copyright registration is very straightforward. So registering your copyrights in your created content is possible to DIY. Whether you're a photographer, an author, an artist, or a course creator or writer, you're creating material that may be registered as your unique, copyrighted material. The moment you create it, you have common law copyrights in the works. More importantly, you can create IP by registering your copyright on your own with the US government Library of Congress. The website with helpful information on how to DIY copyright registration is www.copyright.gov/help/faq/faq-register.html.

Second, for most experienced businesses or serial entrepreneurs, trademark registrations can be done yourself. You'll need to know how to describe your goods or services and differentiate from prior filed or existing trademarks that appear to be similar to yours. That way, you won't try to register a trademark for something that you can't. You'll also need to keep up with the trademark maintenance schedule and paperwork deadlines as you try to secure the registration and then keep your trademark maintained properly. Check www. uspto.gov/trademarks/basics for more information.

One note on trademark registration and DIY. The email you list and the mailing address you provide for correspondence communication by the USPTO will be spammed. There are many instances of entities that email and send hard copy mail to your address that appear to be from the government but that are not in any way associated with the government. These are all scams and spams. So you may wish to use a PO box and provide a designated email to receive the scam and spam materials. In no event should you remit payment for these scams and spams. The USPTO will never email you requiring that you submit payment for your pending trademark listing. I have even received inquiries from experienced businesspeople and companies with the scam materials attached, questioning if there was a payment required. They look official, but they are not legitimate.

If it's not clear to you by now, let me say it outright: All IP is pay to play. This is crucial to remember. You're entering into an exchange with the government for exclusive rights that may be valuable but that are dependent on the quality of the submission and the expertise with which they are created. Never in twenty-three years of practice as an attorney have I seen anyone successfully DIY a patent that became a valuable asset. Consider this: If you believe that this patent asset will be one of the most valuable assets in your business and that it will have a multiplying effect on your business valuation, then why would you DIY? The more you're staking on a patent, the more reason you have to hire a professional, experienced attorney who will do it properly. But as we've learned, you need to be well equipped for engaging that IP attorney; you need to be proactive and know what to avoid and what to ask them.

Broken Record

It doesn't matter if you work with me or my law firm, just *don't do it yourself.* You're better off burning your money for entertainment, as mentioned earlier. Filing your own patent not only wastes time, energy, and money but also will put you and your business at risk of not creating the real wealth and value your business could have in the future. And you may even cause the consequences of ruining your business operations entirely.

Your idea is too good to throw away. Do it right the first time and rest easy knowing you're protected with quality assets that contribute value to your business now and that create future value that can have a multiplying effect if you sell or license later. The peace of mind alone is worth the cost. And you can do business for the long term knowing that your IP assets typically appreciate over time and can even create the opportunity for you to exit by selling them or your entire business when the time is right.

CHAPTER 4

IP MISTAKE: FILING FOR EVERYTHING

I n the early 2000s post–dot-com era, a software company hired me to help them with their patent portfolio. When they handed their portfolio over to me from a big law firm, I found they'd already filed over two dozen applications. They had no idea what was covered and what wasn't. All were currently pending, with nothing even reviewed by an examiner, much less approved to be granted as patents. It was my job to assess what they had, determine what was important or valuable, and, in short, untangle the mess and help them maintain and create valuable IP assets.

To get started, I wanted to understand how the company saw each patent application working as a business asset. The problem was, they didn't know. They had filed for these patents as protection for whatever they thought was unique, often right before a software release, not really considering how they would use them as assets within their company. Patent pending status had been good enough to raise venture capital investment, but now they needed to know if they were worthwhile or just another expense. The growing number of patent applications was becoming a cost that was great enough to understand whether it was worthwhile.

Most large companies do not know what all their patents cover or how they are used (or will be used) as business assets. Start-ups and early stage companies need to know this before they file, because they have fewer resources to begin with, and every asset must contribute to the value and growth of the company.

This situation is not unusual for large companies, or even midsize companies. Each division within a company often has their own patent portfolio. The person managing each division is not aware of what's happening in other divisions from an IP standpoint. There are many inventors; some leave the company while the patent application is still pending. And the overwhelming majority of those patent assets—by some accounts 98 percent or more of patents—contribute no return on investment (technology transfer offices of research institutions and universities are often worse than that). Most companies don't know what they have, and nobody else knows, and it doesn't seem to matter much. Because more filings are better, right? Not necessarily.

Consider the giant. IBM is known for having the most patent filings and/or granted patents in the US year after year. They reportedly earn $1.5 billion or more per year in patent licenses. That's unusual among patent licensing deals. Their vast portfolio attracts new, innovative hires and customers alike. Even so, while this revenue is compelling, the vast majority of IBM patents are *not* commercialized, meaning either they are not licensed, nothing is done with them by those who do license them, or both.

Within other large corporations like IBM, most do not know what patent assets are in their portfolio or how much of their portfolio they use in the business operations or for revenue or impact in any way. Henry Chesbrough's research in open business models shows that most companies he surveyed used only 25 percent or less of their patent assets in connection with their business operations.[1]

Few companies can operate like IBM. Generally speaking, having ten patents is better than five because it means you have more assets. But is fifty better than ten? Maybe, if you can leverage fifty assets. Is five thousand patents better than fifty? Probably not, because you almost certainly can't leverage them all and most likely won't even know what each asset is worth, or useful for, or to whom. Creating a patent involves a cost. Patenting without strategy can waste resources you could better spend marketing your business or investing in other assets.

As with any potential revenue-generating activity, perform a cost-benefit analysis. More is not always better.

Don't File for Fun

Most patents have no commercial value. When an inventor wonders, *Will anyone pay for exclusive rights covered by my patent?*, the answer is probably not. This is true for individuals, for big corporations, and for small and midsize businesses. Usually, smaller companies cannot figure out on their own which inventions are worth the time, energy, expense, and legal analysis required. They don't have the budget to waste money on patents with no likelihood of success or return on the investment to create those patent assets, and they cannot afford to file everything. I'll often talk to a small business owner considering forty (yes, *forty)* possible patents, when two, three, or four is all they need. I know this because that's what the data says—patent research and analysis tell me where they'll get the best return on investment (ROI) for a lower cost and less amount of time.

---

1 - Henry Chesbrough, *Open Business Models: How to Thrive in the New Innovation Landscape* (Boston: Harvard Business School Press, 2006).

Remember that time is money, but time is time. Your inventors' best use of time is creating content, developing software code, designing products, leading a team of engineers, business development, sales and marketing, and more often than not in start-ups and early stage innovation-based companies—a combination of these activities that only they can do. So you have to factor in that their time cannot be devoted to doing this research and analysis for patentability or for writing the patent applications—except to the optimal, limited extent needed to communicate with a proactive, experienced patent attorney who can translate what they already have into the patent application that will be valuable in their business.

Larger companies have a different problem. They typically have no idea what's in their patent portfolios, which patents contribute to direct revenue versus marketing, or anything else about their patented assets.

My post–dot-com software client was acquired for over $200 million in cash and stock. But when my firm began to work with them, my assessment revealed that fewer than *half* of their pending patents had anything to do with their current or planned software offerings. Apparently, any time an employee had an idea, they filed a patent. Nobody asked if it made sense from a business point of view. No one asked how it was or would be connected with product or service offerings. Or how it would block competition. If the company doesn't ask, the outside attorneys will not likely ask either.

My client realized they had to change their filing strategy—from filing everything to being more selective and using data to drive their decision-making. From then on, they would file only for patents that were offensive (meaning they offer that software or service or plan to) or defensive (meaning they would block a competitor from obtaining exclusive rights to something valuable).

They'd already spent a fortune on patenting with no ROI (except checking the diligence box to confirm they had patent applications when trying to obtain funding) and couldn't afford to bleed more money without confirming value or expected return. Let this be a reminder of the importance of patent research and strategy. If you cannot indicate how filing the patent application (with the expectation of receiving exclusive rights, confirmed by data) would be useful to the business, don't waste money that you could better spend on product development, marketing, or expanding commercial footprint in the market. Filing patents just to file patents is merely an expense, not an asset creation activity.

Keep in mind that not every good idea is a valuable asset that deserves a patent. "Is this patentable?" is the number one question new clients ask me. Answering the question accurately requires research and analysis of the prior art, as discussed earlier. After having conducted research and analysis for more than two decades as a patent attorney, and analyzing them as a patent examiner before that, it usually takes only a consultation to determine whether what they are disclosing is likely not to be patentable. If it's something I've already seen, it's not patentable. The differentiation is key. This requires patentability research and analysis and at least one interactive session with the inventor(s) to pinpoint the heart of the invention, which is key to patenting.

And it takes only a few questions to understand how valuable it would be to their business if they could be successful in securing exclusive rights from at least one patent. But I can usually tell them up front if an idea is good or not. But a good idea does not mean a good investment.

Business owners who learn about IP for the first time often experience the pendulum effect. "Let's file for everything!" You might have felt that when you picked up this book. And you've probably got excellent ideas that warrant patents. But don't try to patent everything just yet. Not everything is worth patenting. Make sure you figure out where your best ROI exists.

Assessing Your IP ROI

Perform a cost-benefit analysis on every invention and patent just like any other business asset. Filing for everything means you'll run out of money, time, and energy. Don't spend yourself out of business.

Run the numbers by gathering the IP research and analysis as well as other market and business data. As you examine your data, ask yourself the following questions:

- How does this (potential) IP compare to my competition?
- How big is the impacted market for it?
- If I had exclusive rights to keep competition out, what would that be worth?
- Am I more likely to close deals as the exclusive source on this?
- Will I get better pricing for my company and my customers?
- How impactful will this product or service be?
- How long will I use it?
- How quickly will technology or science evolve from here?
- What does higher (value-based) pricing do for me?
- Is this a commodity yet? Could I secure a patent *and* a trademark?
- Is there anything that could be trade secret and maintained indefinitely?
- How will I protect and enforce the IP?
- What about cybersecurity?

If you don't know what you have or how it's useful in your business, you can't do anything with it. With a cost-benefit analysis, at least you'll know your ROI before you start investing in the IP.

How to Know When to File

Think of the previous questions as gates that follow stages of activity. Your idea needs to travel successfully through each gate in order to ensure that your filing makes sense. If your idea fails any of the gates, stop and select a different idea to test. Just like with new product development, IP asset development needs to be assessed and reassessed at different stages with decision gates, all supported by data and analysis.

The business gate comes first. Is this product or service valuable to the business? If you can't earn money, and if you'll be spending your marketing money on the patent, you might hamstring your business by filing.

The market gate is second. Does this product or service have competition? What do they do? Does this product or service contribute to differentiation? If yes, move on to the next gate.

Is this idea associated with a future product or service? Think about differentiation *and* competitive advantage. Just because you can get a patent doesn't mean you can manufacture it or that people will pay more for it. It may be new and unique, but will your customers or clients perceive the higher value?

Only after passing these gates do you assess the patent gate. Within the various IP protection systems, it's important to be clear about whether this idea is patentable, possible to keep as trade secret, or to register as a trademark or copyright. Or just publish to block others from doing the same.

The problem with file-first business leaders is that they skip all three of these questions, resulting in many failures and a lot of wasted resources. Idea documentation and filing are not enough. Do your research (if you have expertise in doing so) or pay a professional research team or IP attorney who is proactive, experienced, and cares about the impact on your business.

In one case, we tried to support a start-up technology company that was developing a wearable device. We conducted patent and trademark research to support their innovations, and the path forward seemed clear, as long as they took the time to differentiate from the closest prior art when creating their patent application. But they decided to forgo following our advice and pursue their work without following a patent strategy—they just wanted to check a box and proceed without building the quality asset and without investing the time to ensure that the application was aligned with their business and differentiated from competition. They wanted to do everything at the lowest cost, regardless of following strategic advice to create high-quality assets.

A Sample Cost-Benefit Analysis

Let's say you've developed a medical device. If a patent gives you the exclusive right to sell it, you won't be concerned about lowering your price to compete with other vendors. That means the higher your product's quality and the effectiveness of the inventive solution, the more the pricing of the end product can be associated with the value it provides.

Now let's say you're in consumer electronics, and you've developed a wearable device for health and wellness. Maybe your device recharges faster. Maybe you've developed a better battery. That gives you a competitive edge you don't want anyone else to duplicate. You're no longer competing with commodity pricing. You have a superior product with features that customers value and for which they are willing to pay a premium.

Next let's say you have invented a product feature on a flashlight that is sold at your local Walmart. That single feature may be represented in several patents, especially in a competitive field like flashlights. If you're charging five dollars for a product that's barely differentiated from your fifty competitors, and customers don't really care which one they buy, should you pay thousands of dollars to patent your product? Maybe not. Even if most of your competitors are not patenting, at least one may be. Consider the MAGLITE flashlight. They've secured hundreds of patents and enforce them vigorously against competitors that try to introduce low-cost products, whether in physical stores like Walmart or online. If you don't have patents to cross-license when they sue you for infringement, you're finished. All you have is cash to settle the dispute. Who wants to give cash to their competitors?

Yet there are many cheap copycat or knockoff products (especially in consumer product areas), where the manufacturers or distributors make no effort to invent, differentiate, or even patent on their own. They may save money in the short term but may eventually be shut down for infringement—especially in a highly competitive, highly innovative space where there are many patents owned by many companies. So using data to determine whether to file patents, and whether you can avoid infringement, is essential to effective decision-making.

Now we'll say you've invented a biodegradable plastic container, but it's five times more expensive than other containers. The market may not bear that cost today, so a patent may not make sense. But with changing economic, social, and environmental pressures or regulations, in the future there may be advantages to having the biodegradable solution. That advantage is multiplied if you have exclusive rights to make, use, and sell that invention in the marketplace. So patenting may benefit your business in the longer term, even if not immediately.

This is why you need to conduct both a business analysis and a patent analysis. Just because you can patent an idea doesn't mean you can make that patent worthwhile. Just because you could get a patent doesn't mean it's a good product.

Work as a Team, Not by Yourself

If you're a business owner, patenting is not just about you. If you're the only person looking for IP ideas in your company, you may miss your best assets. Even small and midsize businesses need to consider promoting the ideation process and at least awareness of IP assets.

Getting everyone in your company to think about inventing or creating IP assets in the smartest way takes a culture change. By raising your company's awareness of IP, you'll shift every employee into a culture of innovation. It changes the mindset to identifying problems and trying to solve them. Encourage the team: "Stop and ask yourself if you are solving a problem in a unique way related to the product or service. Is anyone else doing it this way? Is it better? Is there value here?" Raising awareness and rewarding innovation will create a culture of searching for solutions and finding hidden assets in your company. If an idea can be IP, can it be an asset? Foster this open, encouraging, contributory environment in your company.

In one example, before their acquisition, CNET created this company-wide culture of IP awareness and stimulating innovation and inventive problem-solving that contributed to the success of the business. They developed a reward system to encourage invention disclosure and those inventions selected for patenting. In another example, the national labs of India needed to foster a new perspective on the importance of inventing and filing patents, so they created a program to stimulate invention disclosures and reward patent filing. These types of approaches are useful if a company has never explored IP or actively created IP assets. However, they ultimately need to be balanced with the ROI assessment—from the business and the IP legal perspectives and with data to ensure that there are valuable assets created rather than merely increasing the number of patent applications filed.

This is where many nonprofit research institutions and university technology transfer offices fail—organizations whose job is to bring inventions to the marketplace. Typically their approaches are to encourage or require invention disclosures. And typically there is little or no prior art or patentability research and analysis or business/market analysis conducted in advance of deciding whether to file a patent application. They try to keep costs at a minimum, so they forgo these key steps in the stage-gate process of ROI assessment. They have no way to ask and answer questions because they're not selling products or services—they are not closely connected to commercialization; they identify problems, obtain funding for research, publish results, and often file patent applications. The overwhelming majority of these types of patents never make any commercial impact. The solution: evaluate every disclosure before you file; make an assessment of the likelihood of success for ROI; and invest in creating quality assets that corporate entities will value because the exclusive rights are commercially impactful.

So this section is one of balance. Yes, incentivize your employees or research teams to be aware of and to look for inventive solutions that may have commercial value. They might bring you a goldmine of ideas. But assess the value and likelihood of success with creating patent assets before you file patent applications. Or they might bring you a money pit of costs.

Take Notes

Document and discuss your ideas and creative, inventive solutions to problems because they may be or become potential IP assets. In a small company, the CTO, R&D, the COO, and even the CEO or cofounders or owner(s) can be responsible for reviewing documentation. Don't rely on your memory; write it down. Ideas become reality when we speak them and write them. So document them in an idea journal (digital or traditional) without judgment at the time. Inventors (and especially software developers) tend to edit or judge ideas and conclude they are not patentable because they were simple—even though they solve important problems and do not exist elsewhere. Communicate ideas within your team. If you can't communicate it, you can't file a proper application. If you can't file properly, you can't secure a patent. If you can't secure a patent, you can't create an IP asset. If you can't create an IP asset, why are you innovating? Someone else will do the same thing. Where is your competitive advantage?

In my experience, software developers tend to be documentation-averse. If you're a software developer and you're not writing code, then you're not being productive, right? But the documentation is also important because it allows others to understand the code and its functionality, to improve on it, to debug it, and to deploy it effectively. To address this tendency with software companies, at first (but now we use it with all clients) we developed an interactive stage that we call invention capture to make it easy for inventors to provide details around their ideas and disclosures without requiring them to document everything, given all the other work they have to do. We discovered that it reduced friction in the patent process and made it easier to communicate with clients to understand the heart of their invention, differentiation, and business goals for the patent assets before they had to invest in having us draft and file their patent applications.

A cybersecurity client showed me a five-page patent filing when I'd expected forty. I asked, "Where's the rest of the story? Why this patent? Why now? What didn't work at first, and what makes this different? Where are the use cases? How is it used?" No one had asked those questions—either within the company or with their outside IP attorneys. So their application was thin, lacking important details about functionality, differentiation, and connection to the commercial implementation and alternatives.

Nobody likes documenting their failures or problems. But it's essential for patent applications. Showing the roads you traveled and the work you put into testing, experimentation, and trials to realize your final product is part of your narrative—your patent story. So when you work with a patent attorney, tell them the good, the bad, and even the ugly parts of your story. Then what's important for patentability, and differentiation from expected examiner prior art rejections can be included to create a high-quality patent application.

Quality assurance is essential, but many people prefer not to do it themselves. If that's you, a patent attorney can do it for you. You don't want a gap in the origin story of your patent, copyright, or trademark. Cover your bases by hiring someone to double check your work.

Choose Carefully

As I've mentioned, quality beats quantity. It's better to have one huge filing with lots of detail, data, and use cases than a dozen failed filings of five to ten pages each.

Minimum filing requirements are *not* minimum requirements to secure a patent. It's like writing a book. A typical nonfiction book is forty thousand to seventy-five thousand words. You could write that minimum word count and produce a book . . . that nobody reads past the first chapter. And if *you* think it's a good book, you'll waste money marketing it.

Even if you manage to secure a patent or trademark with a five- or ten-page filing, you may learn too late that it doesn't cover what you'd hoped in terms of exclusivity, your company valuation, or enforcement.

Who does your patent keep out, and how? Your goal in creating IP is for it to be valuable, to be connected to the company, to be linked to your products or service, and to keep out competitors.

CHAPTER 5

IP MISTAKE: WAITING TOO LONG TO FILE

IP filing is a race. The first person to file and get accepted wins and can shut you down, even if the idea was yours in the first place. Waiting too long means you don't get a patent. Too many companies do just that.

At the time of this writing, I'm working with an early stage start-up. They have raised capital, but they've been putting off filing their IP. Most start-ups, particularly those in biopharmaceuticals and biotechnology, do exactly this—wait to file. Their founders believe they need an inciting event to file patents, trademarks, and copyrights, such as a certain amount raised or revenue goal achieved. But to get those customers or build that minimum viable product worth investing in, you need to launch your product or service, which means it's public use and therefore now unpatentable. And that bars you from filing.

I get it—validating your product as early as possible is good business sense. You want cash on hand to build yourself a buffer, and you want customer excitement to show to your investors. You're conscious of how you spend those first precious funds—capital raised, revenue generated, or both. You may feel tempted to forgo filing because you're afraid you'll need that money for something else. But waiting for launch isn't smart for building IP assets, and there is no second chance. You've got to patent inside the correct time window, or you're out of luck.

Consider this case. An inventor in wastewater treatment technology worked with us to secure a quality patent application. We always advise to have a continuation practice. This means that when you have a first (parent) patent application allowed, we file a continuation (child) patent application that claims priority to the parent filing date. This allows for improvements to be patented without having to patent over your initial invention. Because without this continuation strategy, your initial patent will be prior art to your future improvements or modifications. Just like with early filing before public use or competitive filings, continuation practice must happen before a trigger event. A patent issuance is that event. After the initial patent issues, you cannot create the child or continuation filing to keep the priority claim.

In the wastewater treatment case, the inventor decided not to file the child/continuation application. Not even a few years later, he had made an improvement that he wanted to patent. But now the initial patent was prior art. And that was the closest prior art. This makes patenting much more difficult. There are approaches to deal with it, but they can take your enforceable patent off the table and cost more time and money than committing to the continuation strategy. Most inventors make improvements. And most patents are improvements over what existed before. So expect it. Commit to it. Create a more valuable portfolio.

Luckily, it's easier than ever to test, prototype, and assess before you launch—without barring yourself from filing. You do *not* have to launch your thing to confirm product-market fit. You do, however, need to keep everything you're up to confidential, which we'll talk about more in chapter 6. Software developers are the worst about jumping ahead. They usually justify waiting to file by telling themselves, "But we're in beta, so it's OK." Not if the public is using your software. If no confidentiality, noncompete, nonuse, and other legal essentials have been signed, then that minimum viable product of yours is now in public use. And that means no patent for you.

Again, we'll get into confidential beta testing soon enough. For now, what can you do to vet the market before you launch?

Prove a Patent Is Worth It (or Not)

First of all, if you haven't yet, run the numbers. Open a new spreadsheet. What's the projected profit? How much market share can be captured? Is the patent worth doing? Let's say the patent process, from first conversation with an IP lawyer through patent secured, costs $20,000. Is having that patent (or family of patents) worth *more* than $20,000? Few lawyers ask clients these questions, and even fewer business owners and start-up founders answer them for themselves.

If you don't know what the ROI on your patent will be, of course you'll prefer delaying your filing. It's simply a legal expense, not an investment you expect to add a digit to your company's validation, which it can. So many business owners don't realize how valuable an idea can be. If they don't understand how an idea can become an asset, they don't file. And they lose out on the best applications of their ideas because they thought they could make a quicker buck selling a product or service.

Filing itself does not have to be a loss of money and time. You can use the filing process to deepen your understanding of your idea's value. That can put money in your pocket later on. Here's what I advise all clients to do next, once they've run the numbers.

Research the Market, Derisk the Patent

Most people don't do this patent research because it's hard, confusing, tedious, and time-consuming. For me, it's fun. I'm an information nerd. In another life, I would be running a market research firm. You might even say I already am . . .

The patentability research you do before filing is equal if not superior to the typical minimum viable product research process. Are lots of companies filing in your area, or just a few? What has already been published? Doing some basic research is like checking the wind in golf to know if you have the right club.

Bring your patent idea to USPTO.gov—this is a free, searchable site for patentability research. There you'll find two databases worth searching, USPTO Patent Full-Text and Image Database (PatFT) and USPTO Patent Application Full-Text and Image Database (AppFT). These are for issued patents and for patent applications still pending review, respectively.

USPTO Patent Full-Text and Image Database (PatFT) is helpful for sorting ideas quickly and searching the full text of all patents. It also provides all the information you need about the IP. For most products, I recommend sticking with dates after 1976. But if you're improving on something basic like a hammer or a toothpick, you may also want to search between 1790 and 1975.

USPTO Patent Application Full-Text and Image Database (AppFT) also shows you what pending patents are in queue. It's helpful for making sure your new idea isn't too close to someone else's. You don't want to get halfway through the process only to find someone else filed just before you and got accepted.

You can get myriad data from these two resources. So that you know how to use the databases, let's look at a simple patent idea example—cell phone cases.

Alternatively, there are other free sources for patent research, like Google Patent searching. Explore. Find what works best for you if you choose to research on your own.

In my experience, most inventors' DIY search results conclude that there is nothing like their invention, or there are many, many patent documents like their invention. Neither is usually correct. I advise using a professional, experienced patent attorney or legal team to assist you with the research and analysis; or find a software solution that is accurate and thorough, like our Patent Forecast software (patentforecast.com).

Prepatent Filing Idea Validation Example

Look at your current cell phone case and finish the sentence "I like this, but the problem is . . ." Maybe it's too bulky or too rough on the hand or it's not reflective enough to spot in dim light. Doing that same assessment with any product or service gives you an instant idea for a new IP. You just need to articulate the problem.

This approach is useful for all companies. You file a patent for the same reason you start a business—to solve a problem. Solving a problem no one else has solved as well as you have and in the same way as you have derisks your filing.

You have to know how your solution is sufficiently different from and superior to other products. For example, what if your cell phone came with both a typical case *and* a screen protector? That solves the problem of a cell phone case that does not protect the screen from cracking.

How do you know if this combo case protector is worth buying? Well, are other companies filing patents for a solution like that?

You'll never find *nothing* in the patent office's databases. Someone somewhere has filed something similar enough that you'll make a connection. Nor will the potentially thousands of patents you find look exactly the same. You need to sift through the noise and see if anyone is doing what you're proposing.

Keep in mind that patent filing is just exchanging documentation for a unique solution with the federal government for exclusive rights to sell that solution. The government guarantees your protection under their patenting system. It doesn't mean others can't improve on your idea and file their own patent, but they can't steal your idea without violating a government agreement.

You're probably wondering by now how to use the USPTO databases. It's a straightforward process at the start but quickly becomes unmanageable if you're doing all the research yourself (companies hire NEO IP for everything you're reading about now).

Let's say you want to get your patentability research started on your own. Great! To begin your USPTO-enabled market research, pay a visit to the PatFT (http://patft.uspto.gov/netahtml/PTO/search-adv.htm) and the AppFT (http://appft.uspto.gov/netahtml/PTO/search-adv.html).

Search for both issued patents and patent pending applications using keywords in the "Terms" box and choosing "Claim(s)" in the drop-down field. Consider searching names of your known competitors to see what they have filed as well. You'll be amazed by what you can find and by the new ideas you can get from looking at other peoples' concepts.

For example, going back to our phone cover idea, I searched "Term 1" *cover* with the drop-down field set to "Claim(s)" and "Term 2" *phone* with the drop-down field set to "Claim(s)" and found 2,689 results! And the search was only able to load patents that were issued since 2001.

You want to use each of these tools so that you can search both the patent pending and the successful filings databases. Even a narrow search will often show tens or even hundreds of thousands of results. You're dropping a dart from a helicopter hoping to hit the bull's-eye somewhere in the city below. Those are the odds of your patent filing being accepted as sufficiently differentiated from all other filings in existence. That's why a patent lawyer can cut through this extensive research and find the exact data you need.

Now consider this. Just because you *could* do this market research yourself does not mean you should. In fact, I highly recommend against DIYing *all* the research because you'll be looking only at your idea's patented competition from your perspective. A patent attorney thinks like an examiner to anticipate which combinations of already patented features, functions, and components are close enough to yours to trigger a rejection. That's why you need another point of view.

The patent office will reject you if they can. My firm once worked on a patent for a sleep apnea product that solved the problem of masks leaving lines on users' faces. The examiner initially denied the claimed invention because "a firefighter's mask is close enough." Because we had conducted the prior art research effectively, drafted a patent application that included differentiation from relevant prior art, and had experience working with challenging cases to successful issuance, we were able to help this client secure the patent as well as the continuation practice that allowed the client to secure more claims beyond the initial allowance.

A DIY approach would not have ever considered searching for other face masks outside of the sleep area, and it might have been stuck at the rejection. But we argued that the examiner's reply, which Frankensteined other patented products together, was nonfunctional and therefore could not compete with ours. By positioning the application to be differentiated from relevant prior art ahead of time by doing sufficient research to differentiate our filing, and knowing what was not relevant or what were applicable references, we could address it in our reply.

What's the firefighter's mask equivalent for your product? You may not know yet. You probably don't. And that's OK. Patentability research often blows clients' minds for two reasons. One, they had no idea that planned features of theirs already exist on other patented inventions in a different industry, and two, thousands of patents and applications reveal a significant opportunity—where they *can* file a patent and get approved.

When It's Not Too Late

In most cases, it's not too late for your new idea unless you've gone to market. Anything already being bought and sold is prior art and therefore ineligible for a patent. But not getting the patent doesn't have to be the end. Chances are you already have new IP candidates. What's the next generation of your idea? What does your beta test feedback say (see chapter 6)? What new features and functions have been planned but *not* deployed?

You can patent over yourself as long as you're innovative. Treat your minimum viable product as prior art. That way, your main hurdle to acceptance is just making sure the next version of your product differs sufficiently from your existing product.

If you still believe you can DIY patentability research and analysis, I encourage you to try it. I think you'll soon change your mind. You have better uses of your time, like creating and marketing new ideas. Pay the specialists to do the hard work for you. They'll think of important points you would otherwise miss.

It's important to note that not just any lawyer will do. Some patent lawyers don't even do the research we talked about. You tell them your idea, then they draw up the filing and submit the application.

They may not even consider prior research, which isn't much better than DIYing it. In fact, I'd say it's worse because you're not only out the time but also you've lost money paying lawyers who will not secure you a patent.

Don't be careless with your best ideas. Pay a competent attorney to help you derisk your inventions and give them the best shot you can at becoming an IP asset. Play it smart, then enjoy the profits. You reap what you sow.

CHAPTER 6

IP MISTAKE: THE OWNERSHIP ASSUMPTION

Who owns your intellectual property?

It seems reasonable to assume that if you create it, you should own it. But what if you hire someone—an employee, a contractor, or a vendor—who works on your invention prototype? Who builds your app? Who designs your company website? Assuming it's "yours" may land you in a sticky situation. That's what happened to a high tech life science data company whose owner reached out to me.

The company had developed testing protocols and algorithms unique to their business. Automating the way they did things would streamline employees' workflow, improve productivity, and therefore increase revenue and profit. But they're a life science company, not a software company, so they hired a third party to develop the necessary software. But they failed to ask an IP attorney to review the contract.

The executive team assumed that by paying for the software, the company owned the deliverable—a software unique to their market and business. But once the software was finished and deployed, my client caught a rumor that their vendor tried to license the software to their competition.

Imagine their shock and outrage. I reviewed the development contract and found that they had failed to include an assignment clause. The data company had, in writing, agreed to purchase a *license* to the software. They had it built from scratch, and all they got was a license. You may consider that sneaky on the developer's part. Yes, it is. And it's also a failure to do due diligence: *Read. Before. You. Sign.*

That's what this chapter is about—what needs to be in your contracts before you sign. Otherwise, what's yours may become theirs.

Even if you paid for it.

The Assignment Clause: Own Your IP from Day One

Copyright belongs to whoever created the thing—the software, the website, the manuscript. An *assignment clause* allows creators to transfer their rights, benefits, obligations, and duties to someone else, such as a customer.

That contract between the life science company and the software developer did not contain an assignment clause. This meant the software developer held the copyright to the software *simply by creating it*. The payment for the deliverable was for the license when it should have been for the copyright ownership as well as for any and all other IP associated with it, including any improvements.

So without an assignment agreement with a contractor, a license and the deliverable are all you get when you pay someone to code, create, or otherwise do work for you (unless you agree otherwise in writing). This client got to use the software the developer delivered, but the developer appeared to be free to license or even sell the same software to anyone they so choose. And it was perfectly legal to do so—except for the confidentiality clause they signed in the original agreement as discussed previously.

Avoiding this kind of issue—preventing a vendor from selling what should have been your IP to competitors—is not the only reason we're debunking the ownership assumption. Consider this case. A nonprofit organization had a complicated donor-facing website. They hired a developer to create it with unique code to meet their requirements. When they needed to update it but maintain or improve the functionality, the vendor who built the website gave them unacceptable terms, attempting to charge them a significantly higher than market rate. So the nonprofit reviewed the contract to see what recourse they had. And that's when they realized they didn't have ownership of the code or the visual presentation of the website. They had a license and the deliverable. This presented two nonoptimal choices—rehire the vendor anyway under expensive terms, or build a new website from scratch and include a work-for-hire agreement with assignment clauses to ensure that any and all IP is owned by the organization, not the vendor.

I could not stress this enough if I tried: *You need an assignment clause in every agreement you have with any third-party contractor or vendor as well as with all employees.* This is so important, it should be placed at the beginning of the relationship. Ensure no one else but you owns your IP.

The assignment clause simply states that you own anything you pay the vendor, contractor, or employee to do. The critical phrase is "agrees to assign and does assign"—that is, the vendor, contractor, or employee must assign the copyrights (and other IP) of anything they create in your work-for-hire relationship to you, their customer, client, or employer. Unless an assignment clause is present in the agreement, all you get is the license. The vendor or contractor, and possibly the employee, owns the IP.

Most of the time, companies aren't aware of this problem until it's too late. This doesn't mean it happens to everyone or that most vendors or contractors you hire are out to get you. Experienced service professionals and agencies typically include assignment clauses in their contracts already to provide the ownership of IP to reside with the client or customer. Otherwise, they'd have lots of angry customers. However, if you don't have an assignment clause in an existing contract, and if the other party is agreeable, address it and fix it immediately.

In the emerging marketplace of apps, SaaS, online side hustles, and digital IP, establishing ownership is a must. The assignment clause helps ensure you own your IP—but it's not the only clause you need.

The Four Nons: Keep Your IP Yours

In addition to the assignment clause, you need the four nons: nondisclosure, nonuse, noncircumvent, and noncompete. Include these in all contracts, not just those relating to IP. Let's go through each so that you can see why.

Nondisclosure Clause

A nondisclosure agreement (NDA), also called a confidentiality clause, is an agreement to keep certain information confidential. Trade secrets, proprietary processes, or anything else that gives you an edge in the market could be included.

My life science data client did not have an assignment clause in their contract with the software developer. Fortunately, they *did* have a nondisclosure provision. It required the vendor to refrain from disclosing any material that the company transferred to them to any third party.

That's how we got them out of their sticking point. We considered all communication between my client and the software developer as confidential. I stamped all copies of communications with the vendor as confidential and sent them to the vendor.

By notifying the vendor that the information is confidential, we were telling them to treat it under the terms of the nondisclosure clause, keeping them from leaking the company's trade secrets to my client's competitors. The nondisclosure clause also prevented the vendor from licensing the software to anybody else, as doing so would violate our contract. With that hook, we managed to pull the life science company's IP back to safety.

Confidentiality is for companies of every size, from sole proprietors to corporations. A small business needs an NDA to use with potential collaborators, manufacturers, distribution partners, and others. Any company trying to raise funds would also need an NDA with potential funders. This agreement keeps their IP safe from unscrupulous companies seeking to undercut their competitive advantage.

The Race to File

Many start-ups, student entrepreneurs, and bootstrapped small business owners decide to just build and release their product without considering IP. They don't realize that by taking this approach, they risk losing their rights.

In the US, you have one year after publishing to file for a patent. Giving a presentation at a business pitch competition counts as a publication. Launching a website. Providing demonstrations at a trade show. Speaking at a conference about your innovation. One year later, your would've-could've-should've patent enters the public domain, and it's too late to file. Remember, someone's always out to knock you off.

Small and midsize companies will often go to a trade show, hold demo days, or reveal their prototypes. Suddenly a large company contacts them to learn more about their invention. That same week, the large company files a patent application for an improvement on that invention. Without an NDA, the small company has lost control of its IP.

An NDA may keep your IP from leaking into the public domain. Under an NDA, alpha testing, beta testing, and conducting a prototype presentation are not considered publication or public use. Your disclosure, discussions, or demonstrations under the NDA are confidential. You hope that they also prevent the recipient from "stealing" your IP in any way, but keep in mind that NDAs can be difficult to enforce. In any case, NDA documentation is essential to preventing issues with your presentations becoming prior art to your own applications.

At some point, you have to bring your IP to market. And with that NDA, you can keep testing and presenting your innovation until it's ready. Just remember that it's still a race to file, so the sooner you can secure a priority filing date with a quality patent application, the better.

Two-Way NDA

When you present your IP to a third party and ask them to sign your NDA, they may ask you to sign their NDA, too. This is called a two-way NDA.

A two-way NDA is especially important if you are a smaller company doing business with a larger company and you don't need anything from them. You don't want the burden of knowing what a bigger company or competitor knows, because then you have to keep that information confidential.

An NDA keeps others from claiming your IP as theirs. To keep them from *using* your IP, you need a nonuse clause.

Nonuse Clause

You don't want recipients of your proprietary information using it for any reason. A nonuse clause prevents them from using your IP internally (think larger companies), even if they do not disclose your IP to any third parties. You still don't want them to use the disclosed information or your IP for any reason except for the reason you're discussing with them (investment, business collaboration, license, etc.).

Here's an example. You are a small company doing business with a large company. The contract has an NDA but not a nonuse clause. The large company may adhere to the NDA by not disclosing your information to someone outside their company, but they use your idea internally for competitive advantage. They may compare it to internal documents or projects to explore how to compete with you. You only realize this when they release a product with features you developed. By then it's too late for you to do anything about it.

A nonuse clause shields you from other companies, regardless of their size. Starting a clause with "except for the explicit purpose of doing business with us" in your contract protects your IP from being used by someone else.

Even with an NDA and a nonuse agreement, you don't want the receiving company using any of your information for any reason except one that benefits your business. That's why you also need a noncircumvent clause.

Noncircumvent Clause

A noncircumvent clause keeps what's yours, yours—even if you have not formally filed a patent. It's intended to prevent the recipient from trying to design around or work around your disclosed information—your IP.

This clause's absence is most likely to cause you problems if you're a smaller company doing business with a larger company. The larger company could take your IP, make some minor changes, and create a new product. They didn't infringe on your IP; they took your idea and figured out an alternative. Suddenly, instead of having a lead in the market, you have a new competitor.

I had a client in the wireless communications field who developed a product. We didn't want them disclosing information a potential vendor could exploit for a competitive advantage over them. That's why we included a noncircumvent clause in their contract.

So far, we've protected you from external parties. But to keep your own employees from leaking your IP, you need a noncompete clause.

Noncompete Clause

A noncompete clause prevents former employees or contractors or even vendors or other business partners from competing with you for a reasonable period of time in a reasonable geography or scope.

The definition of *reasonable* is critical, and it varies by state. For example, California does not recognize the noncompete clauses generally. So be sure to seek legal advice from a competent attorney in your state or the state in which you are doing business. Many companies, particularly internet-based businesses, don't operate in only one state. They deal with people everywhere and seek customers anywhere. You need to talk to a legal professional who can help you figure out what *reasonable* means in your specific situation and what other state laws apply to clauses like these.

Let's look at how a noncompete clause works in the restaurant business. Suppose you employ a manager who knows all your "secrets," from recipes to customer service. If you don't have a noncompete agreement, that employee may try to open a competing restaurant or work for a competitor. Your restaurant's name, signage, and menu can be recreated in close proximity to your own. Worst of all, you can't do anything about it—unless you have other IP, including trademark and copyrights. Trade secrets can be valuable IP. But only if you identify them as trade secrets and only if you can keep them secret (including using agreements with employees to take reasonable steps to maintain the confidential information).

Training key employees might include exposure to some aspects of trade secrets, like sharing recipes that cannot be reverse engineered, primary market research that is used to create proprietary pricing models, special vendor relationships, customer contact information, and other items, and it only makes sense to equip them to provide the service you need. However, it exposes you to problems later on if you don't have a noncompete clause (and the other non- clauses described earlier). They can quit and tell competitors, media, or any random person, "Here are their *real* margins."

What do service professionals like plumbers and landscapers compete on? Relationship, pricing, and customer base. Once everyone knows their competitive edge, what do they have left to differentiate themselves from others?

Let's be realistic. Your employees are going to leave for various reasons. And when they go, is the IP in their brains yours or theirs? Make sure you own it, because you are the reason it exists. Don't let your IP walk out the door every day without ensuring that you have the right agreements in place to protect it.

At least the government is on your side when ex-employees try. The Obama administration's Defend Trade Secrets Act (DTSA) gave US trade secret enforcement a big boost (and real teeth for enforce-ment). Employers began applying the DTSA immediately after its passage. For example, some companies filed lawsuits against auton-omous vehicle engineers or key employees who left and went to competitive companies. The suits alleged that these employees took trade secret know-how to their new employers. Even in California where noncompete clauses are not enforceable, DTSA was one way to fight this issue. No one wants to deal with trade secret or IP theft or misuse by former employees. But without key agreements and clauses, you could have problems beyond your control.

Get your brand trademarked. Register your copyright. File your patent applications. Use the non- clauses with vendors, contractors, and employees. Make sure you own your IP. These steps will save you from headaches and heartbreak in the long run.

Protect Your Innovation

I have a good friend who is an IP attorney in Silicon Valley. He has been known to say that many big high tech companies do not originate their own innovations. Where do ideas come from in Silicon Valley? Forty percent are internal (to the big tech company), 30 percent come from small companies that pitched to you, and 30 percent come from companies that pitched to venture capitalists but didn't raise enough money or their businesses failed for other reasons.

According to this math, more than half of the innovation in Silicon Valley big tech companies originates from smaller or start-up companies. But they lack infrastructure, capitalization, and a customer base. They need to reach out to larger companies to try to partner for resources or distribution; they need to pitch to raise funding and promote their products and services.

Here's where the four non- clauses come into play. If you're fundraising, ideally you want to have taken steps to protect your IP rights by making the appropriate patent filings and so forth. Additionally, you would like to require agreement to the four non- clauses by anyone you pitch to. Otherwise, they could take your idea and run with it. Instead of you profiting from your hard work, they do. Realize, of course, that not everyone will agree to sign. You have to navigate the risks and consequences of business and continue to make progress toward your goal, even if there is no way to guarantee protection—or success. Because there are no guarantees. But protection with IP rights and these non -clauses can help manage the risk.

The same goes if you are in talks for a merger and acquisition deal. During the due diligence process, you tell the other party every-thing about your company, including your IP. If the deal falls through, the four non- clauses protect your assets. You won't have to worry about the counterparty taking your IP to increase their competitive advantage—or at least you have it documented and can prepare for enforcement if needed.

As with most documents related to IP, it's against your best inter-ests to DIY the four non- clauses. Just like DIY for your patents. Here's why.

Don't Let Your Assets Leak

I get it. It's tempting to search the web for free generic contracts. But those agreements are not developed for you, and you don't know what you don't know. Not only that, but laws vary in different countries and even in different states.

For example, European privacy laws differ greatly from those in the US. If you operate across different geographies, you must have clauses to cover different legal environments.

Don't DIY your standard agreement, or you'll risk losing every-thing you've built. Get a contract that suits your needs. Have a professional do your contract so that your assets don't leak out. You can commission a contract template and adapt it to different situations, but you must get an expert to do it for you.

Remember, your contracts must have the five clauses: assignment, nondisclosure, nonuse, noncircumvent, and noncompete. You need these clauses written separately for you *and* for your business, as your business may have different assets that need protection.

If you hire others to do work for you, you need a work-for-hire agreement. This agreement, which all contractors and vendors must sign, also needs all five clauses. Everyone has a side gig now, so you need to be clear where the line is. You need that clarity whether or not you own what you're paying for. The agreement should cover not only the deliverable but also the rights to the deliverable. The rights must be assigned appropriately.

Also include all five clauses in a work-for-hire agreement for use with full-time and part-time employees. In addition, your lawyer can add a disclosure clause stating that if employees develop IP, they have to tell you about it. Otherwise you won't know they've developed something worth copywriting, trademarking, or patenting, which could affect your business down the line.

If a vendor you're considering requests that you sign their standard client agreement, *read the contract!* Too many people sign paperwork without reading it first. If you find comprehending legalese a challenge, or you just don't have time to, hire a lawyer to read contracts for you. Otherwise, you may be giving away royalties, revenue, or rights.

You may think you'll work it out later. Yet you'd never think about not paying for health insurance because you don't need it right now.

Once I privately invested a five-figure sum in an early stage company. It was a no-brainer for me to pay a corporate and securities lawyer to review the terms before signing. It costs a few hundred or even a few thousand dollars to ensure that the tens of thousands of dollars are well placed and with the proper or appropriate clauses. It's just good business sense not to DIY when there are clear assets at stake.

By hiring a lawyer, you're paying for expertise to guide your agreement with terms. Almost like insurance on your business. Is that worth $500 an hour to review an important contract? Absolutely.

And if you don't like the contract a company asks you to sign, negotiate new terms. Both sides should agree, not just the party who created the contract. Most businesspeople are reasonable. If not, that may be a signal not to engage in that relationship.

Note, however, that I'm saying *people* are. Which brings us to a difficult conversation I've had with many clients over the years.

The Ethics Conversation

If someone can get away with it, will they?

The answer depends on the person. Unless we're not talking about a person at all. And that's a difficult concept to grasp, so let's try our best.

Here's a cold, hard fact for you:

Companies Are Not People

It's unethical for people to take your ideas without your permission. But companies are not people. A company contains layers of people with different levels of authority. It's not a person unless it's a sole proprietorship. The good, smart people you're working with may have integrity, but those people might leave that company. Tiers of an organization don't stay consistent over time. And companies are acquired by other companies that have different cultures and ethics.

Many companies are accountable to shareholders. In that environment, profit is elevated over ethics. If something is not in writing, it doesn't exist. A patentable creation is not *your* invention if you didn't make sure you own it in your contract. It's *theirs* because *they* can make money off it to pay dividends to *their* shareholders.

Consider the case of a researcher who had signed a license agreement with a technology company. The researcher had contributed a product to the company and had signed a royalty agreement with them.

The technology company was bought by a larger company. Later, that larger company was bought by an even larger company. When none of the people who the researcher made the original agreement with were left, the royalty payments stopped. When the researcher sought relief for the contract, the larger company refused. What could she do? She had only the contract to enforce and ultimately won the payments that were due. But it took years to enforce the agreement because the ultimate "owner" of the contract that she executed with the original company was nothing like the entity she started with.

Consider asking your lawyer to include an arbitration clause to address disputes. These terms help you resolve disputes instead of having to go to litigation in state or federal courts, which can take years and years and cost hundreds of thousands of dollars to conduct. Even then, there is no guarantee how the dispute will be resolved, even if the facts and law appear to support your case. Litigation is far from predictable. Arbitration can be helpful as an alternative.

Relationships also change when one party starts making a lot more money. For instance, a company may claim they're paying a salesman too much in commissions. The salesman can produce a contract showing that the company should pay him more for increasing their revenue.

People who raise money run into this issue as well. They do the work, but the client refuses to pay them. A contract ensures that they are protected.

Never forget that while you work with people, you are ultimately doing business with a company. A company is not a person. You need contracts to guarantee that everyone behaves ethically. But you yourself must also behave ethically. Because . . .

You Are Accountable for What You Agree To

Every manipulation, every lie, every unfulfilled promise distorts reality. By engaging in these actions, the person is distorting their own world. It's like throwing a rock at a glass window. It shatters the view of reality. Now you see liars where you once saw friends because you've become a liar yourself. It is in your self-interest to tell the truth, to keep your promises, and to fulfill your agreements.

You are accountable for what you agree to. One person may not steal your idea even if it's legal. But in a company of fifteen thousand people, it might happen if no one holds them accountable. Foster a culture within your organization for everyone to honor their agreements. And those who don't will stick out. You'll see them . . . if you care to look.

People Tell You Who They Are

The best defense against theft is refusing to do business with untrustworthy people.

People's actions and words tell you who they are. We get into trouble when we don't pay attention or when we don't want to believe them. A new contractor refused to sign our work-for-hire agreement on his first day. He thought it was unfair to assign IP rights for his work to us, given that he was very smart and clever and had a PhD. This told me that he was going to withhold his contribution to the company, even if I could explain why it was important and even if he signed it. He was letting us know that he had a moral dilemma in assigning his ideas and IP to our firm. I thought that hiring him under those conditions would be unreasonable to us, so I didn't.

Learn from the times when you have been cheated or stolen, but don't let it be a burden you carry with bitterness into new relationships. Forgive and move on. Learn from the experience. Avoid past mistakes. Get your remedy at law, if you can, learn your lesson, then do something else. Like find someone else. And when you find someone else to work with, don't project your past experiences onto them. Remember that you're the common denominator here.

Hire the Right Person

Hiring is hard. Letting go is harder. It's far easier to hire the right person from the start than to hire the wrong person, realize they're a bad fit for your company, and then figure out how to let them go.

To work with my law firm, Neo IP, you need to be smart, curious, creative, proactive, and a team player. It doesn't matter if it's a position for an attorney, an agent, a patent technologist, a scientist, a technical writer, a paralegal, or an assistant position. We need all five qualities. I have learned over the years that if we like someone because of their technical or scientific degree, but they lack any one of those five qualities, they will not work out long term. You need to have all five at our firm.

We work with creators in a team environment and help them develop valuable assets for their businesses. We help connect them to the resources they need to make a positive impact with their IP and with their businesses. Will you be a good fit if you're not a team player? No. If you're missing even one of the five qualities, it's not going to work out.

When you know what you want in a new hire, the hard part gets easier. And when you know how to protect your IP, you don't have to learn the hard lesson. But knowing how to keep your IP safe doesn't mean it *should* become IP. Ideas, after all, are potential IP assets. By themselves, their value is zero. This may be hard to believe, especially if your business's numbers are impressive. But you will. After you read the next chapter.

CHAPTER 7

IP MISTAKE: THE GET-RICH-QUICK PATENT FANTASY

What if one patent equaled $1 million?

Many people have this fantasy. They treat patents like million-dollar lottery tickets. You file, you win. As with the lottery, however, the odds are stacked against them. Within most companies, creating a product or service that enjoys exclusive rights or licensing the IP to others fails to earn an ROI some percent of the time. Not all patents or IP assets are quality assets that have value in the marketplace. This should come as no surprise to you by now. Most patents are half-baked and poorly researched, if at all, and not well filed, or the invention is not valuable in the marketplace. While it may be patentable, it isn't profitable because there isn't an addressable market willing to pay for that solution.

Consider this case. An entrepreneur with a scientific background and track record of raising venture capital investment at high levels invented a solution to kill bacteria and even viruses. This sounds incredibly useful in today's ongoing pandemic situation. He successfully secured dozens of patents and raised significant capital to launch the business and scale from early research to prototypes to commercialization. He also scored a meeting with a Fortune 100 CEO to discuss a partnership or joint venture. But his ROI for those patents and that business: zero. When confronted with a term sheet for the business deal, he decided it was worth billions of dollars, not millions. The F100 CEO discontinued discussions and the deal fell through. No business deal can happen if the terms are not reasonable. The value of the patents is determined by data and ultimately by what another company will pay for them, or it is based on what value will be returned from their use in business. It's not determined in isolation. Most entrepreneurs and businesses overvalue their IP because they aren't using data to inform the valuation or because they aren't considering how the market will value it.

Now consider a major source of patent filings: research. Fewer than 5 percent of technology transfer patents earn a return on the investment to create those assets; in most university research technology transfer offices, they never realize any return, or perhaps 1 to 2 percent of assets provide any revenue. Without being overly critical of their models, it's fair to acknowledge that the success rate for nonprofit institutions or university research technology transfer is generally worse than corporations. Fewer than 2 percent of inventions become moneymakers. For example, my undergraduate alma mater, North Carolina State University, has a successful program by technology transfer metrics and was ranked number two in the nation for patent licensing in 2020–2021. It sounds high, but the percentage of profitable inventions is still low when considering the total patent assets and the capital investment and time associated with them. The university takes a business-minded approach overall and has more success compared with other institutions. Imagine how much more could be licensed—what if the terms and approaches changed to position 98 percent of patent assets licensed? Imagine the sustainable growth to fund ongoing research and patent asset creation.

As a general rule, universities do not patent with commercialization in mind, or at least they do not follow a process that creates enforceable assets faster, the way that companies, especially early stage or growth companies, would want. Their goal is to keep costs down, not create high-quality assets that consider differentiation and exclusive, enforceable rights that have value in the commercial markets. So to keep costs down, most technology transfer offices file provisional patent applications, then international patent applications under the Patent Cooperation Treaty and delay the US patent application nonprovisional filing. So you've started the patent clock ticking to file in the national phase in specific countries (which can be thousands or tens of thousands of dollars per country) without having derisked the patent application by ensuring that you have success in the US. Remember that by conducting patentability research and analysis and building in differentiation from the prior art identified, you streamline prosecution and reduce later costs and time in moving toward a granted patent. Yet most tech transfer offices do not conduct prior art research or proactively instruct the outside patent attorneys to differentiate from prior art. Also, remember that there are mechanisms to accelerate US patent examination via the fast track—this gives important information about what claims may be allowable, typically in fewer than six months. This helps to derisk more expensive actions like national phase filing in other countries. So the approaches are opposite of what most companies would take. Additionally, many universities, perhaps unintentionally, create barriers to licensing during negotiations, actively discouraging entrepreneurs and companies from licensing their patents or patent applications and making reasonable business deals. Because they're still in line with the metrics that judge their institutions, and this is the way it's always been done.

Some organizations, such as nonprofits and government bodies, conduct research with fewer than 1 percent successful commercialization. Their focus on research with no thought to commercial impact or creating a business case impairs licensability; not that they should be in the business of creating businesses, not at all. But at least create assets that would be valuable to businesses. And without proactive research and analysis, plus marketing, how will anyone find the valuable assets they create? They rely on third parties to seek and find what they want based on what is published. Not a high return on the investment in creating those patent assets.

So how is your patent different? How can you make money? To make money, you need a product that's relevant to the market. But if 95 percent of patents are market irrelevant, how do you know what to license?

Some big companies with deep pockets monetize their patents by suing people. A friend of mine is one of the all-time top patent brokers. He specializes in enforcement licensing, which means suing people to make them license an IP. That's common in the high tech sector.

My patent broker friend told me, "You have to make people pay attention to you. The way you get the attention of your prospective customers is marketing. The way you do that in patents is to sue people." Litigation gives people a timeline to respond to you inside the legal system, forcing them to pay attention to you.

Big companies like Microsoft never voluntarily license anything. You have to sue them and win in court to collect. I once heard a head of licensing at Microsoft say, "Our budget for litigation is infinity." Unless you're a large company with deep pockets, litigation is not a viable option.

I don't litigate to create value. The best way to get ROI on your patents, and IP generally, is to make and sell a product or service and enjoy the benefits of exclusive rights. It's a limited monopoly you get the right to enjoy: no direct competition for what's covered by the IP, value pricing, exclusive contract awards, and so on.

If you build it, they almost never come—despite what most independent business owners think. Having a patent puts you in the history books, but it guarantees you nothing else. So how can you enjoy a return on your hard work? Let's explore some options.

Increasing Profits and Protecting Your Patents

We live in a specialization economy, at least in the US and developed markets. This means you don't have to do everything yourself to make a positive commercial impact and realize revenue for your contribution to products and services. You can work with third-party vendors at every step of the way, from idea to IP to prototype to product. The reach inventors and companies have today through the internet and technologies allow for rapid prototyping, contract manufacturing, marketing, distribution, and even digital collections for payments. It's never been easier to build and sell goods and services—particularly if you take the right actions at the right time.

Patents are assets. They can still have intrinsic value, even if you fail to commercialize them. Someone else can buy or license your patent. After the 2000–2001 dot-com bust, many companies closed, but their patents remained. Venture funds and companies that had security interest in patents sold them, even though there was no operating company—no commercial goods or services connected with them.

By many accounts, fewer than 5 percent of currently filed patents are high quality and make any ROI to create them. These are the patents that enjoy a high ROI. If your patent is created intentionally and informed by data, differentiated from prior art, and detailed with alternatives, then your patent may make it into that 5 percent. Even a little research can go a long way, if you do it in advance of creating the asset and if you're guided expertly. And it's easier than ever before. Again, you can begin doing some of your homework even before hiring an attorney.

I'll tell you a quick story. It seems unbelievable today, in 2022. I was a patent examiner in the mid-1990s, and online patent research did not exist. While the USPTO had databases and digital copies of patents, they were not readily searchable and were not available to the public on the internet. As a member of the public, you had to physically go in person to the USPTO main office or to a USPTO patent repository library at select universities. North Carolina State University was one of those repository libraries in the mid-1990s. You searched on a DOS-like interface to receive a listing of patent numbers that matched your query, then you had to walk into rooms of microfilm and microfiche to find the corresponding reel and frame number associated with your patent numbers. One by one, page by page, you could read individual patents in scanned electronic form—and print them for twenty-five cents per page to analyze later. The internet wasn't really a thing then the way it is today. Even as a patent examiner at that time, I had to physically go into a file room to search manually for patents—from hard copy printouts of them. There were little drawers (called shoes) stacked full of patents categorized and subcategorized in various ways. If you were searching for a patent that another examiner in your group was using, then it was not possible to find it. Imagine how that affected searches and results during that period. Searching on the USPTO computer system was optional. It was mandatory to search the hard copies.

The *Official Gazette*, a booklet mailed to patent attorneys, gave notice of published patents. To *research* the patent itself, you had to go to one of about a dozen patent repository libraries in the US, or to DC to obtain the microfilm or microfiche. Many companies and law firms would hire former patent examiners to do this work for them because it was exceedingly tedious, made efficient only by experience with particular subject areas by people who had worked there and had familiarity with those documents.

By the late 1990s, the USPTO.gov website launched a fully searchable free patent database. Hallelujah! Now anyone in the world can research US patents. Constructive notice is given automatically, electronically to the world every week when patents are issued on Tuesday, and publications go out on Thursday. Unlike Google Patents, which is delayed by about three weeks, this government database is kept up to date because they are the source of the publications.

I reference the US patent system predominantly because it has historically been the most active patent system globally, with about half of all the patents filed annually coming from individuals and entities outside the US. The US has been number one in patents because of our laws that recognize property rights and that have a long record of valuing IP rights as largely predictable and enforceable. China has surpassed the US in total patent applications for the last several years, but this is in part because the government requires Chinese inventors to file there before filing anywhere else. Notwithstanding the number of applications, the quality of patent assets in the US is still recognized as being more valuable than anywhere else. Besides our rule of law recognizing IP rights and property ownership, the US market for products and services is large, and so the IP rights in the US affect a valuable commercial footprint.

Remember, having a patent means nothing unless you use it and look after it.

Keep Off My Patent!

A well-researched patent application that sufficiently differentiates from prior art may not be a lottery ticket. But if and when the patent office grants you the patent, it basically becomes a deed. And as with real property, if you don't make it clear it's *your* land, well . . . others may trespass.

Think of your patent as your front lawn. The term *patent pending* is a KEEP OFF THE GRASS sign. It gives you the right to build there. To effectively keep out trespassers, show up on the porch with a shotgun. In the case of patents, you need lawyers to litigate for you, or you must partner with a company to enforce your patent. Let's explore this in greater detail.

Be the Ring Doorbell

Patents are like a Ring doorbell: You can see if someone steals from you, but you cannot prevent it. It's surveillance, not security to enforce your rights.

In the same way people advertise their Ring or ADT security at their house, you can advertise the fact that you have patents. Mark your territory on your website, on your product packaging, in your marketing, and on other online media with "Patent Pending" or "Patent [Number]."

Monitoring your market to see who may be infringing on your patents is like competitive intelligence. Competitors may not always come from inside your market. More than half of all products and services in the US are from outside the US.

Luckily, it's easier than ever to monitor your market. You used to have to visit trade shows and ask companies who's pitching and selling to them. Today, you can automatically monitor your competitors' websites, social media, press releases, and conference presentation videos from the comfort of your phone. Be aware of what your competitors are publishing. Listen to your customers, partners, and friends. If they're buzzing about competing products online, pay attention.

Patent data changes like the weather—it's not at all static like a landscape. My firm, Neo IP, uses our own proprietary and patented Patent Forecast software to monitor the changing conditions of the patent space every week. Because patents and publications become prior art, after you file your patent, other companies may cite it. Look for forward citations to see who is referencing your work. That may be someone trying to build around you. At least it tells you that they are investing in patent applications that are trying to improve on what you've done or are related to it enough to be worth watching.

Be the Ring doorbell of your market and watch what's happening in your yard.

Put Trespassers on Notice

What if you catch someone on your IP lawn? Your next steps depend on what kind of company they are.

Shutting down patent trespassing by an early stage start-up is pretty straightforward. You're probably not going to sue them because there are no profits and no damages. Most early stage companies can't litigate their way out of an infringement. That's why small companies usually don't sue each other. It's a huge distraction and expense.

You can put smaller, newer companies on notice in a soft, friendly way. Say, "I'd like to make you aware of our patent in this space. We take IP rights very seriously, and we welcome an opportunity to discuss a mutually beneficial collaboration. How can we resolve the trespass?"

The smaller they are, the more effective a single notice letter will be. Everybody wants to do business, so know what you want out of the deal ahead of time. You could order them to cease and desist. Or you could charge them a royalty through a limited license to let them stay on your property.

Don't send a cease and desist letter to a large company. It won't end well (in the next chapter, I'll explain why). If you absolutely must send a cease and desist letter, get a lawyer to do it for you. Keeping the tone friendly may solve the problem.

Enforce Your Assets

What if the trespassers don't comply and you do have to litigate? The Bible says to count the cost and consult your many wise advisors before you wage war. Patent litigation is a war. It takes a long time. It's draining and distracting. Know what's at stake before you fight.

Litigation funds offer you loans to help you fight for your patents. If you own high-quality patents in a high-revenue marketplace, defend them as best you can with whatever weapons you can get your hands on. Talk with litigation firms and interview more than one lawyer to find a good fit. Hiring the wrong counsel means spending lots of money and certain loss. Hiring the right counsel still means spending lots of money to *maybe* win.

That's why you need an enforceable asset. Few patent filers think about that when they file. Almost no firm does what we do, which is to think ahead. How will I use this asset? What if I have to enforce it? How would someone design around my patent? Ask yourself these questions during the planning process (see chapter 2).

If the trespasser can invalidate your patent by citing prior art that you overlooked, this makes your patent become worthless. You don't want your patent invalidated. By considering prior art, design alternatives, and litigation during your patent research, you can avoid this. Because you've been reading this book, you've already planned as though you might have to enforce your patent from the beginning. You have created an asset you can enforce. Most patents that reach litigation are high quality.

There are more resources available today than ever before to patent owners to fund litigation to enforce quality patent claims against other companies that appear to be infringing. Patents are big business. So if there is enough impacted revenue from quality patent claims, funds will back the enforcement litigation to secure their ROI through the licensing revenues. On the other side, there are more companies that exist that may be hired to try to invalidate your patent through prior art challenge. You can imagine why the patentability research and analysis at the start is more valuable than mentioned previously; it may determine the outcome of your enforcement. If you have not conducted the research and rely only on the examiners to identify the prior art, then you have exposure to validity challenges when you try to enforce your patents.

Most patent owners don't know what their patents do and don't cover. You need effective, open communication with your patent attorney to make sure you do. The story of your patent is its potential, and what's covered in the patent itself are the claims. The claims are what you enforce.

Selling Your Patent

In real estate, no one cares about a little strip of land in the middle of nowhere. The key is location, location, location. And timing. The same goes for your patent, whether you commercialize your invention or not. If you have a lot of property you don't plan to develop, then you can sell it. If you can't make something of your patent, someone else might. But how do you find buyers? Who cares about your patent?

Before you think about selling your patent (by itself or with your business), ask these questions:

1. What's the market for your idea?
2. Who are the companies in that market that might pay for your idea?
3. How similar are they to you?
4. Does anyone else have patents similar to yours?
5. Is your patent or patent application a quality asset?

The last question is extremely important. If you DIY or file on the cheap, you'll get a low-cost, low-quality patent that won't make money. Ever.

Buyers will not come to you. You have to be proactive and reach out to them. Our Patent Forecast software provides dynamic visualization to show who else is investing in patents around you. From this data, you can build a list of possible licensees or potential acquirers. The bigger the company, the more valuable the exclusive right to your IP will be if the claims are solid and the patent application is high quality and differentiated from prior art. The largest company may ignore you. But the second, third, or tenth largest business may find your patent valuable because they would value your exclusive rights versus their competitors. They may not care about your company, but they care about how they can exclude their competition.

Another great candidate to consider for a sale of your IP assets or business is a competitor that does not have any patents. Your patent may give them a competitive advantage; depending on the timing, especially if they have litigation against a competitor, they may pay a premium for it.

Consider the example of Google's acquisition of Motorola Mobility; they paid a premium for the company only to secure the IP rights and sell off the operations. Also consider Google's acquisition of Nest for over $2.3 billion. Nest developed its own IP assets along with products and operations; Google/Nest later sued competitor Honeywell over years and ultimately realized a settlement and cross-licensing for the fast-growing smart thermostat market. Consider even more recently the Google acquisition of Fitbit, which led wearables patent assets and had a solid commercial market position. Google lacked the patents that Fitbit held; by acquiring the company, it acquired the market and the patents. With the Google commercial footprint and resources, these IP assets are even more valuable than they were in the hands of the companies that originated the patents. Notice a trend here?

How do you begin to market your IP? Create a package to feature your patents, detailing the size of the market and your IP. Provide data for context to confirm the quality, scope, and priority for the market, which are all indicators of value. Summarize it and use visuals to facilitate communication of your IP position. Use industry terms rather than repurposing the patent abstract. Include patent and market context data so that potential customers don't misinterpret your marketing collateral as a cease and desist letter. Discuss the competition around your patent, presenting it as a market opportunity.

Here's an example. One of my clients developed text and mobile privacy software. It's helpful for managing enterprise communication by blocking access to websites, people, and other companies.

We developed the patents, and my client tried to make deals with large companies in the telecommunications sector, companies like AT&T, Verizon, and T-Mobile. To show the context for their patent, they discussed the growing smartphone market in their package. They found a channel partner who helped a larger company acquire the client's patents and other business assets. How? They knew the market, so they knew which companies might have the most interest.

Most deals aren't made at auction but by soliciting multiple companies on a reasonable timeline. Often, your neighbor buys from you. The typical review time for a company to decide whether to buy from you is sixty to ninety days.

The company acquiring your patent usually takes all the IP, including patents, trademarks, and copyrights. Sometimes they won't use everything in their business. You may still see more opportunity, and you may want to retain rights or a license to build on a part that's unrelated to their business. But usually the buyer wants everything. Many times, even if the seller has a holding company for the patents and an operating company for the business, the buyer won't just want a license. They bundle all the assets into one entity because it's more valuable to control them that way.

A Few Reminders

Don't think of your patent as a lottery ticket. If you bet on luck, the stats are against you. Patents can be a realistic way to convert ideas into money. Ron Harrington of the Harrington Group became a billionaire by transforming his ideas into IP, then into products.

Before you draft and file, research the value of the space around your patent. Are there other companies there already, or are few investing in that area? How necessary is your property going to be? How useful is your solution? One of the first things I ask clients is, "How do you plan to use your patent if it's successful?"

Combined revenue and profit with IP rights is the highest revenue multiplier for anything you could ever want to sell. Build your company around patents, and the company will grow even more profitable.

If you're just going to talk about it, don't file a patent. If you put in only the minimum effort, it's a waste. But if you do the research and see potential around your IP, build it. They may not come, but you can go to them.

Like Cinderella, you have only a limited time to act on your patent. Those who are intentional and persistent enjoy the reward. It may not be a jackpot worth billions, but it may be *something*. And that's better than 95 percent of everyone else.

CHAPTER 8

IP MISTAKE: OVERLITIGATING (AND UNDERLITIGATING) PATENT PROTECTION

In the last chapter, we talked about the friendly cease and desist letter. What if you get a refusal or no response? Tread carefully, or you'll find yourself in a legal minefield. Here's why.

For decades, sending cease and desist notice letters was common when you suspected infringement, hard evidence or not. Then case law changed. Now you no longer want to assert that someone is infringing on your patent because of the possibility of a declaratory judgment suit. That's when the other party claims that you (wrongly) threatened to sue them for (nonexistent) infringement.

To be fair, you *could* send that angry letter. "We'll litigate!" And you can mean it. But now the other party can sue you right back for threatening a lawsuit. Worse yet, they can take you to court in *their* jurisdiction. They get the home court advantage, which may be the deciding factor depending on where the company potentially infringing on your IP does business. For example, if a company in Northern

California is in your space, never, ever send a cease and desist letter. Northern California is notoriously hostile toward patent owners.

In contrast, I know several patent owners filing suits over infringement in the Western District of Texas because the local laws ensure that suits proceed rapidly and fairly and that they particularly favor the patent owner and its IP rights. It's difficult for the plaintiff to ask for delays, and that helps the patent owner, who wants to resolve the dispute more quickly.

Still, why play the odds? An aggressive, accusatory, insult-laden letter is a distraction at best and a trap at worst. So I advise clients to keep the stern letter gun in its holster, and I don't recommend litigation unless absolutely necessary.

The best way to use your patent is to build it into a product and sell it, enjoying your exclusive rights, as covered earlier. Mind your business, grow it, and prosper. Usually, most competitors will mind theirs. Most companies don't willfully or intentionally infringe on other companies' patents anyway. If they do, it may likely be a big tech company. Tech Bro culture is infamous for IP free adoption, which often goes unpunished because the perpetrator is too big to sue, or they reside in a territory unfriendly to patent owners, like the Northern District of California. Coincidence? Maybe. That may be how the situation feels, at least, and I pray you don't find yourself having to make that call. We try to keep our clients out of court, but if you need to enforce, you must proceed with an informed position.

What to Consider before Litigation (or Settlement)

If you do need to litigate, lead with the desire to resolve everything as quickly as possible. The larger the company, the deeper their pockets. It's not reasonable to imagine that a small, innovative company will outlast the big corporation. Time favors money. And money can create more time—that is, defendants like to stall proceedings and delay the trial.

How much time, you might wonder? Typically, it takes six to twelve months of internal document-gathering before your own litigation counsel is prepared to file the lawsuit. And after the complaint is filed and served, there are another six to twelve months of exchange with the opposing party and the court before anything happens, whether that be the initial lawsuit filing, motions to dismiss, counterclaims, dispute settlements offered, and more. And even then, the latter result is overwhelmingly likely—by some accounts about 98 percent of IP infringement suits are resolved by settlement. Both parties reach an agreement.

The exceedingly high percentage of settlements has an obvious explanation. In general, companies don't want to litigate—like you, they just want to do their business. If they're reasonable people, they'll be open to a mutually agreeable resolution, such as royalties or a business collaboration. The most common resolution is a payment in exchange for a license or covenant not to sue. Another resolution is that the larger company buys the smaller company. If you litigate your patent against a larger company, the larger company may want to just buy your company—as long as you have other assets that are valuable to them.

In any case, your best defense is having high-quality patents that incline the other party to settle out of court. Here's a quick story.

One company took several competitors to court over suspected IP infringement. It was obvious even to consumers that they were all infringing on the patent owner's space. That company held over fifty patents, with priority filing dates from the early 2000s. Although my firm doesn't litigate, we support and coordinate with litigation firms because clients must have the ability to enforce through litigation if necessary. And that's OK with me because the client didn't need to.

Within one month of filing the lawsuit, three of the infringing companies offered to settle—to resolve the dispute without an expensive, drawn-out legal battle. One of those businesses explored discussions for an offer to buy the company's business outright, IP and all.

This quick resolution, while inspiring, is uncommon. After those six to twelve months of just getting your side ready for the legal battle, you can expect three to five more years for the actual case to reach resolution in a district court. And if you try to enforce in court, you can expect your patents to be challenged for validity at the USPTO in inter partes review challenges, usually over prior art that was not considered.

A notable exception to this timeline is any case filed through the International Trade Commission, which protects businesses and individuals with IP rights from imports outside the United States. Let's say someone is importing a product that infringes on your patent, and you file a suit against them. By statute, the entire process from filing to resolution must be resolved by the International Trade Commission within eighteen months. That fast time frame is good for the patent owner, and in the best case, the outcome may be an injunction. That's where the other party must discontinue their business, but they don't pay you any damages. If the injunction is likely, that's motivation for any company to settle the dispute (and pay to settle and acquire a license to resolve the matter so that their business is not disrupted).

Why is injunctive relief so important? Remember the BlackBerry (RIM) litigation with NTP? RIM was facing injunctive relief that would have required it to cease all business in the US for the infringing services. The settlement was $612.5 million.

In US courts, the best lawsuit outcome is damages, but sometimes you need the threat of injunctive relief to achieve the monetary settlement that the patent owner is seeking. So naturally, it's on you to prove the infringement's monetary impact, which means hiring experts. Expensive experts.

If your patent is not unassailable, meaning it's sufficiently written to block competitors out of your space and prevent loopholes and work-arounds, you don't need the experts. You don't need anything. Because you don't have a case. I keep bringing up this point because it's so often ignored until it's too late—*if your patent is not a protectable asset, it's nothing.* A tiny patch of brown grass and no road access is not worth defending to the death. Yet most patents are the equivalent. Most companies don't realize that's exactly what they have until a merger and acquisition deal or they are considering litigation. By then, it's too late. If you have a high-quality patent, you already have what you need to file a suit and win—or better yet, settle out of court.

Why Defending a Patent Is Like Applying for One

I've already hinted at what a high-quality patent looks like. What I haven't brought up yet is worth going into now, and you'll soon see why.

Even if your patent application does everything right, including demonstrating how your patented invention is defensible in court against infringers, your application is likely to be rejected. Patent examiners typically reject first filings because they have limited time to review all the prior art compared with your claimed invention. They have deadlines and incentives to advance the case to a disposition (rejection or allowance), and there are penalties if they allow patent applications that should not be granted. Some might say that's the government for you. But if we want to win this game—and receive that patent—we have to play by the rules, but understand what the issues are behind the scenes, or on the back end. And ensure that you are prepared to win the allowable claims at the USPTO, but also ensure that your claims will withstand validity challenges in the future if you must enforce your IP rights in court.

Filing for a patent is like trying to get a book published. You might face many rejections, and that's OK. You have to keep at it until you succeed.

I usually tell clients that approval of the very first patent application without any rejection is not really a good sign. If the USPTO isn't pushing back at all, then you've built the fence around only a small part of your property. You want to protect your *entire* property. Don't leave assets on the table.

If the patent examiner rejects your first attempt, you get to respond and argue your case. If at that point you receive a second rejection, that response will come through as a final office action. Even then, it's not final. It's not unusual to have two or more exchanges with the patent examiner before identifying what claimed material is allowable.

A similar process of application, rejection, and response happens when you apply for third-party help from a litigation fund if you need to defend your patent but don't have the legal budget yourself. They may also reject you on the first or even second attempt due to the potential risk. Again, that's OK. There is no perfect asset, but many are better than others. You need to show that your asset is worth the risk—that it's so good, infringing competitors will regret they ever found their way onto your turf. Your asset will withstand validity challenge and your claims will be shown to be infringed, with addressable market and impacted revenue that ensures returns to the litigation funder.

So What Should You Do?

We've covered your two options to enforce that KEEP OFF THE GRASS sign—seek settlement or consider litigation. As you might expect, what *you* should do is not a fifty-fifty toss-up.

I help clients decide what to do by considering how much money is at stake, both from current customers and from the total addressable market. If the stakes are $100,000 or less, you need to push hard for a settlement, because both sides will spend more than that on litigation. If you've created high-quality assets and you're active in your market, smaller companies won't want to fight you. Litigation is a war. Your lawyer will want a reserve of capital they can draw against, meaning you'll need an initial retainer of at least $50,000 for IP litigation.

During deposition or interrogation in a lawsuit, the other party's arguments may make you doubt the quality of your patent. That's normal. A litigation specialist I know once told me, "The company you're suing goes through the five stages of grief: denial, anger, sadness, negotiation, acceptance. You don't want a crap patent; you want a patent that makes competitors say, 'Crap.'"

Try to avoid litigation, but remember that your patented assets are worth fighting for—*if* they are worth fighting for. There are no patent police. *You* have to monitor the market and enforce your rights—*if* they are worth it. And if you've avoided the mistakes covered so far in this book, they probably are.

Leave the litigation to the experts—let them do the fighting for you.

CHAPTER 9

IP MISTAKE: ASSUMING PATENTS ALONE PROTECT

Did you know that having a patent does not prevent competitors from suing you for infringement? Most inventors don't. And they find out only when they're the one receiving the dreaded cease and desist letter.

Let's flip the script of chapter 8. This time, it's not you who suspects another company of setting up shop in your territory. It's a direct competitor with patents of their own, and they believe this town isn't big enough for the two of you. So then what? Let's dive in.

As discussed in chapter 7, you're expected to be aware of any published patents that have anything to do with the innovation you're up to. Hiring an IP lawyer to do your homework for you all but guarantees your product *does not* infringe on anyone else's patents. Not every inventor, individual or organizational, hires a lawyer. The DIY mistake ripples on and on into the future, affecting patent defensibility, competitive advantage, and cash flow itself. You can't focus entirely on growing a product's revenue when you're stuck in court defending what you believe is your right to sell it in the first place.

The earlier in the product development timeline you conduct what's called clearance research, the easier it is to design around other patents. It's much harder to resolve the issue once you've launched your product and gotten a notice letter.

Clearance research identifies other companies' patents that you need to consider in your design process to ensure that your products or services avoid infringing on the claims of other patents. You need to know what's most similar anyway, for patentability and differentiation in your own patent application, as discussed earlier. If you're in a highly competitive space in which many companies obtain and flex IP, you need to be aware of clearance—even if you don't pursue patents. You'll also need clearance if you're taking venture capital. Investors want assurance that a competitor isn't likely to sue you and shut down your business as a condition for their investment.

Surprisingly, most companies don't do any clearance research. They just operate their business and hope for the best, or they don't care. If you have patent claims on which they infringe, you need to call it to their attention—with litigation.

But if you want to clear the way, you can hire a law firm to do an informal clearance search—no legal opinions, just get the data. As with patentability research, a close cousin to clearance research, I recommend hiring a professional to do it. You don't know what you've missed until it's too late—most companies find out at the worst times: diligence for fundraising or acquisition. The worst-case scenario I've seen so far is when a company unknowingly builds other companies' patented features into their designs, gets sued, and loses everything—having to shut down their business.

You can avoid that fate. Do your homework first to get the all clear on any innovation, whether you want to file for a patent right now or not. Remember that clearance is for the product or service offering you intend to commercialize. Clearance is different from patentability;

the data may be similar but the analysis is different. Having a patent does not mean you might not infringe on someone else's patent.

So don't try to DIY this one. Hire a legal team if you ever receive a notice of infringement. You will need to have a formal legal opinion to shield you from claims that you intentionally infringed on someone else's patent. You may need this even to defend you from false infringement accusations—emphasis on *false*. You may have a patent, but if a feature that doesn't appear in *your* filing *does* appear in someone else's patent, it could mean big trouble. Here are a few tips to prevent that.

Great Design Is Your Best Defense

Let's say you want to launch a software package with some functions that integrate with those of bigger companies, via API perhaps. Your patent can cover your software's functions. But the fact that you have a patent doesn't give you an affirmative right. Remember that patents (and most IP) give you the right to exclude others from making, using, or selling your claimed invention.

Suppose you invent and patent a new mobile app with GPS functionality. With it, you could monitor a third party or let people know where you are. However, if your map software infringes on existing third-party maps like Google Maps, they can still shut you down.

I once met a prolific inventor who has done work with IBM. One of his many inventions was the ellipsis bubble—the . . . you see when someone is currently typing a text message to you. If you build that function into your app, you may be infringing on that patent owned by IBM. Instead of trying to get a license to use the bubble, or using the bubble without permission, you can look at the original patent and figure out how to work around it—and how you can't (and need to license).

It's OK to build on others' property as long as you're doing business with them—for example, as a partner or vendor. The iPhone used to include Intel chips. Intel holds patents for their chips, including the chips in the iPhone, but Apple doesn't have to worry about the patent because Intel is their vendor. If you're buying a product from someone, you have at least an implied license to include it in your product and sell your product—as long as there are no terms and conditions preventing such use (if you have a partnership or other agreement). As with all contracts, *read before you sign.* Know what your rights and responsibilities are before an attorney reminds you in writing via that cease and desist letter.

What if that happens anyway? Even if your lawyer gave you the all clear on design and you've won your patent? What if a big player in your industry smells blood—their own—and is willing to go after whomever wounded their market share, presence, or awareness? These are all good questions, with better answers than you might expect.

Don't Fight Each Other if You Can Work Together

If someone contacts you and asserts that you're infringing on their patent, you'll need a lawyer to shield you from the accusation that you are willfully infringing. Never, ever respond yourself. At the same time, you're not left with whatever your lawyer tells you to do.

If you have patents of your own (which you should), disputes don't have to come to litigation, damages, and bankruptcy. In my experience, the best way to settle IP infringement suits out of the courtroom is through cross-licensing—an agreement between all parties to give each other a license to use their patents.

Cash doesn't necessarily need to be exchanged in such an agreement. Cross-licensing is always cheaper than settling in court or losing a trial. But cross-licensing can take place only if you both have high-quality patent assets that you each find valuable.

Consider this case. A serial entrepreneur started a new company and was deciding whether to file a patent application. His previous company was suing a major Silicon Valley tech company. He boasted about the patent lawsuit with his prior company. But when he sat down with me, he said, "We don't need patents." Then he listed several reasons why he felt they weren't necessary.

I offered another point of view. I reminded him that his last successful company was suing big tech with its patent portfolio. All the other companies active in his market have patents, and they aren't afraid of litigation either. Without at least one patent or even one high-quality patent application, what will you settle with? If one of his competitors sued the new business, his company would have nothing to use for resolving the dispute, except all their cash.

During a litigation with a competitor, if you don't have patent assets to negotiate a settlement, you can't resolve the suit through cross-licensing. All you have left is cash. And it won't cost you $20,000 or even $50,000. Think more on the order of $500,000 to $1 million, depending on the impacted revenue and market.

To keep anxiety in check, let's remember that IP, like all business, is subject to human nature. Someone suing you won't just spend a quarter million litigating. They don't want to just break even, and they definitely won't want a loss. They'll want to make money. If you're an early stage company or a midsize company, settling with cash could mean the end of your business. So don't offer cash if you can help it—offer a deal, one so good they're stupid to refuse. And businesspeople who get patents aren't stupid.

So get yours. Get as many as you need. Because every patent lets you run offense and defense in whatever market and product category you are. A patent provides evidence that you're innovative and differentiates you from the competition. While they don't give you clearance, patents can attract customers, land partnership deals, and settle disputes that otherwise would have burned all your cash.

CHAPTER 10

IP MISTAKE: IGNORING SOFTWARE PATENTS

P atent naysayers won't tell you that software accounts for the highest percentage of new patents applied for and awarded. Yet many entrepreneurs, including three in my local business network, still say patenting software is a bad idea.

All three told me why it was a waste of time to patent their work. And they each had their own concerns.

The first software creator runs a multimillion-dollar business. One of her vendors is a household name social media company, and that company duplicated her company's designs in one of their platform's essential processes. She assumed that patenting her software would be useless against the big social media player's vast legal war chest.

The second creator said, "Nobody cares about software patents. We've been in court five times in the last couple of years just to defend patents for protection. All you can do is out-innovate the competition."

The third creator had yet another argument. "Software patents are a distraction. You need to focus on getting new users and revenue." To him, patents were old-school thinking in a new-school world.

Let's tackle each objection in turn.

"We Can't Fight Big Companies Who Steal Our Patented Software."

Without patent protection, you have nothing except a first mover advantage. If that's the case, your number one competitor will just roll over you and steal your IP.

If you have a patent, big companies may hesitate to steal from you because they have more assets to lose in a lawsuit.

Even the top player in your market has a competitor. That competitor can use your patent exclusive rights to get market share without the legal drawbacks. If you offer an exclusive license associated with your patents, they might even try to acquire you. As previously discussed, large companies may not care about you, but they care about their main competitors, and they want exclusive rights to their markets.

The truth is you don't have to be the biggest fish. You can be midsize and still push back against the big players or partner with one of them. The bigger you grow over time, the more powerful your patent exclusive rights become and the larger your market footprint is. That includes the footprints of the companies that use your software under license.

As always, you must have high-quality patents. When most software creators think of patents, they imagine low-quality filings that don't protect them. If you don't have a quality asset, you cannot expect to have opportunities to license or litigate.

Many small business owners have vented to me that they can't afford litigation. That's what enforcement funding, such as help from your big allies, is for. You can find law firms that handle enforcement assistance and get paid only if they win your case. The catch is, they only work with high-quality patents and big targets.

You can defend yourself against smaller entities by resolving disputes without extensive and expensive legal battles. If a big entity infringes on your IP, there are attorneys and funds available to take them on in exchange for a stake in the settlement or license (in addition to return of their funds). But it all comes down to the quality of the patents.

"Nobody Really Cares about Software Patents."

The big tech players are also top filers of software patents. And patents are a huge motivation for them to acquire your business. Consider the Google examples presented earlier. If you're not in a market first, you must buy; you cannot build patents later—remember, there is no second place for IP.

The common misconception among inventors is that they are responsible for an idea over its whole lifetime from A to Z. In reality, the creator takes the idea to point C before it's acquired. Then the bigger company that bought it takes the idea from C to Z. Or an even larger company buys them and picks up where they left off. That's the natural flow of business.

That means enforcement isn't necessarily your sole responsibility. You're not alone. You need partners. The bigger you grow, the more partnerships you'll need.

Why should a smaller company tell a bigger company they don't need a software patent? Red Hat, IBM, Apple, Microsoft, Google, and Facebook (now Meta) are all filing at higher rates than ever before. These IP rights are valuable to them. How will you succeed if they're not valuable to you? Again, IP rights are often a motivator for acquisition. If you don't have IP rights as a barrier to entry in your space, what will stop these large companies from eating you for lunch?

Every serious tech fund investor knows that patents are necessary. One of the first questions you'll get from a venture capitalist is, "Do you have patents?" Why would any serious person ask that if no one needs patents anymore?

Look at the data. Large software companies file software patents, period. They're some of the most aggressive patenting entities in the US. And right behind the US-based companies (and sometimes in front of them) are the large foreign software and high tech companies with their US patent filings. Everything has some component of software, and much of that software is patented. That's one more reason to treat software patents with the respect they deserve.

"Software Patents Distract from Business Development."

Every year, I talk with several new potential clients who've already gone to market. Many times, some of them make the commercial launch of their core software offerings—placing their inventions into full public use without patenting. As I've mentioned before, they can't backtrack from that position. Now they have become their own closest (worst) prior art.

When investors like venture capital funds and potential large customers ask why they should work with that company, all they can offer is a unique value proposition (marketing) or features and functions that anyone can use later. Even if they are first to market, the next week, another company could innovate on their material or even adopt it with better marketing and sales, and more capital, and take away every customer they have.

Anyone who says patents are a distraction might face a major distraction if a patent-holding competitor, even a small one, sues them. Cash is the defendant's only resource for resolving such a dispute. Assets are resources for settlement, defense, and offense. If you're not patenting, you're at total risk because someone else can threaten your cash supply any time they challenge your claim.

If you're not going to sell your business or merge with a larger entity, you may be enforcing your IP at some point. You are either selling the IP or protecting the IP. Neglecting this fact is bad business that reflects an amateur entrepreneurial mindset with no view of the endgame. While you never want to be in litigation, you need to be prepared for litigation at the time you create your IP assets.

Consider this example. MAGLITE flashlight creator Anthony Maglica is one of the most notorious patent enforcers. If you get in his space, he will sue you and take you out. You might be a small flashlight company with only $100,000 in revenue. He will shut you down because he wants to own that market. He has a valuable patent portfolio, and he litigates to protect it. He's going to run that company till he dies because he's smart and he understands how business works. Take a lesson from him.

The overwhelming majority of entrepreneurs who have successful companies are acquired. Or they IPO. Both require someone to view your assets as valuable in diligence. If you have no patents or other IP assets, you have nothing but your operations, revenue, and profits; these are all important for successful businesses, but when you add IP to the mix, you multiply the value of the business.

If you are a small business owner, you can't or won't work forever. More than 80 percent of smaller business owners want to exit someday to realize the wealth they've created with their businesses. At some point, you'll want to retire. You'll leave it to your children or sell to another company or entrepreneur. Your assets, your revenue, and your profits all matter. What are your top assets? Most companies today have IP assets in addition to any other tangible property. Those IP assets are patents, trademarks, copyrights, trade secrets, and contracts with third parties as well as their human resources in key persons (who are often the source of the IP assets).

Saying you don't need patents when you're on the cutting edge of your industry is foolish. Everyone is filing patents. If you're not, you're going in a different direction from the best players. The IP rights still matter, and they're enforceable and global.

While we're still discussing software, it's important to note that IP rights and patents are not at all in conflict with open source. Consider the case of Red Hat. They have thousands of patents. And they're the leader of open source software and services to support it. We note many open source projects beyond basics, including distributed computing, blockchain, cryptocurrency, and tokenization of assets (NFTs). Patent Forecast data shows that these are some of the most rapidly growing patent application areas in the US system. If you aren't patenting, you're not differentiating and creating valuable assets.

I was speaking with a software engineer recently about his experience building SaaS products. I mentioned patents, and he shut down. "If you're patenting, you're defending the past, and we want to be building the future." He then botched an Elon Musk quote downplaying patents. Of course, Musk's companies have hundreds upon hundreds of patents.

If Tesla hadn't patented their inventions, Ford could build a similar design with their own patented components and sue Tesla. Porsche would sue them. Even little inventors would sue them. Elon Musk used cross-licensing patent assets to "open" electric vehicle innovation by limiting exposure for his company to litigation from other patent owners. This brilliant move eliminated competitive exclusive rights in an area where Tesla imagines its advantage in advanced manufacturing innovations, including robotics, and trade secrets for its battery technologies. Meanwhile, he leveraged other IP exclusive rights like

Tesla's brand, charging network, selling direct to consumers (no dealers), software updates to push new features to cars, data from the Tesla motors network of vehicles globally, and more.

Tesla illustrates what this book is really about—all the business multipliers you can leverage to increase the value of your business once your patent rights and other IP rights are established—especially when combined with the operation of a business with exceptional goods or services. It's about how to use all your exclusive assets to gain more market, get an advantage over competition, and own your zone. That's the power of IP rights as assets in your business.

You might be wondering now what *cross-license* means. Let's discuss it in depth with Tesla as an example again.

Elon Musk's Cross-Licensing Secret

So many people say Tesla is open source with its IP rights (and patents in particular). Anyone can create their own competing version if they want.

Wrong. Musk's car company is not open source. You can create your own version of electric vehicle (EV) only if you have patents properly created to cross-license in this arrangement. If you've acknowledged Tesla's contribution of IP and executed an agreement with them, and contributed your own IP as cross-license, then you can make your own EV.

But you'll need a battery for your EV. And you'll need to charge it. You'll also need a ton of other accessories for functionality and quality of life. Guess which patents you need to pay for after making your own EV from Tesla's open source model?

If you had the exact same idea as Tesla right now, could you win? No, because you're not Elon Musk. And you don't have the Tesla brand. There's not much market space for you as a start-up. And you can't drive him out because Tesla holds IP and is allowing you to use it under the license agreement. If you even thought you would try to make his life hard, you still need the Tesla IP license from him.

That's a cross-licensing deal. Tesla maintains a cross-license that many refer to as an open source deal, but it shields Tesla while managing what the competition is allowed to do. Tesla benefits from your company not excluding them from your space. Through cross-licensing, Elon Musk ensures that you're agreeing with his terms to get into his deal. He owns that zone.

And his competitors know he owns that zone. What leverage do they have to fight back? None. Because Tesla is already winning on multiple other levels. He's coupled that leverage with the patents while advancing manufacturing and trade secrets to stay ahead of competition. He's in a class of his own.

Inventors who aspire to his level know that patents are also great hiring points. Some software companies use them to attract engineers and talented people who want to work for an innovative company.

Elon Musk is one of the richest men on the planet because he understands IP more and leverages it better than any competitor in any space he plays. He doesn't patent everything. He doesn't even patent as much as competitors or tangential market participants do. To achieve even a fraction of his success, we need to be as smart about patents as he is.

Why Patents Make the Difference

If you're not filing patents but your competitors are, all you have is risk. You're taking a huge chance that no one else will enter your space and kick you out. Are you 100 percent sure you can out-innovate everybody forever?

That's the benefit of patents; you don't have to let everybody in. You can let just a few major players in because you want what they have or you don't want to worry about them. Remember, you're not at the big boys' lunch table. But if you partner with their competitor, they'll be worried. Then they'll want to see if your patent protection is strong, or if they can exploit a weakness. And if they can, they will.

If you're active on social media, you've probably noticed apps that enable you to schedule posts in advance. One company in particular I'm familiar with rushed to market without patent protection. Then someone else came along and built a one-to-one app that matched their features, functions, and user interface. In a few short weeks, the new competitors reached five-figure recurring monthly revenue, which far outpaced the original company's growth rate.

Online chatter indicated that thousands of people noticed the unofficial IP theft. In an interview with the first company's founder, he was asked, "Don't you realize your work has been ripped off?" His response: They didn't have any IP, patents, trademarks, or copyrights. Their strategy was to out-innovate them.

That company's situation is dire. Their future is dark. It's heartbreaking.

When a competitor copies your idea, they can run their business without a care. They make money and go on to use someone else's idea after you're long gone. Ideas are worth nothing. IP assets have value to the company that creates them, and they transfer to other companies if acquired. They can multiply the value of the core business.

If you are an entrepreneur or business owner or stakeholder, you probably want to create wealth through an exit someday, which might mean IPO or selling outright. Except if you don't have any IP rights at all, maybe you can't. Who wants to buy a risky business with proven competitors who can freely use everything you create? When you're done, you have to shut down; your business is finished.

Out-innovating your competition is great . . . in theory. But when the endgame comes, you have to rely on protection to move your asset to the next phase. If you can't do that, you've created a temporary cash source, not a money tree. The IP rights in your company are the resource, your lifeline to the next stage, and the multiplier of the value you've created so far by operating your business.

Even turning over your work for someone else to take those next steps can be profitable. Limited exclusivity lets others build on your work under your supervision. But if you don't have IP rights, you have no exclusivity.

You might still think your industry doesn't need patents, or maybe IP rights at all.

While the software examples presented in this chapter may be interesting, what if you don't sell a SaaS? If you have a painting company, for example, you just want to paint—and maybe be faster, neater, and cheaper than the competition. What painter could possibly benefit from IP? Well, imagine that a new technology lets one company paint faster than anyone else, including you. If you haven't been innovating with patents, trademarks, and more, you're all but finished. It's only a matter of time before the patented competition seizes your market share, up to and including your most loyal customers.

What applies to painting and software applies to every industry. To be blunt, if you're building software—if you're building *anything*—and don't patent it, or create IP rights around some aspects of your business that give you competitive advantage, then I don't know how you can compete in the market. You may have a cool brand and some contracts. But if all your competitors are innovating and securing IP rights, where will you be?

You're not playing by the same rules of creating assets that everyone else is. Sure, you might be acquired, but your valuation will be far less than if you had patents or other IP rights. It's the difference between playing to win and playing not to lose.

Err on the Smarter Side

Not everything is patentable. But there are other forms of IP rights, including trademarks, copyrights, and trade secrets.

Think like your competition. If you don't have IP rights, what will prevent them from copying your every move, every product, or every service offering? Why stop at stealing your ideas? They can also steal your employees and market straight to your customers. They can use your words with their branding and take over your market position.

IP rights give you protection from those tactics. And IP rights themselves are assets. When it's time to raise growth capital, you'll have a greater basis for doing so. When it's time to sell your business, you'll have an exit strategy. Your IP can contribute more value than revenue or hard assets alone in your business. IP can also derisk your business.

Remember when Google bought Motorola Mobility? Why would Google do that when they already had their own handset? They did it for the patents. It's the same reason Bank of America has been investing in cryptocurrency-related patents for years, even while their executives disavow crypto as potential fraud or high risk. They'll be cut out of the market if they don't have IP rights to ensure that other companies have to work with them. With patents, they have exclusive rights and can stay relevant in the future, even if they choose not to deploy the new technologies today.

Watch what the big companies do, not just what they say. Better yet, follow their practices. That's how you get to the top, even if you're a start-up or an early stage company.

What if you don't know what the big companies are doing in your space? Or how to replicate their strategies in a way that makes sense for you? That's when you need data and wise advice. That's when you call in a professional. We'll talk about how to find the right one shortly.

SECTION 2

THE PROVEN IP PROCESS

CHAPTER 11

IP ADVICE: DISCOVER YOUR IP'S UNIQUE VALUE PROPOSITION

F or most of the book, I've warned you not to do it yourself. This chapter is different. Here you *can* DIY most of what we're going to cover, even before you get a lawyer.

You know that ideas are free but can become assets worth millions (or more) when the marketplace wants to buy whatever it is you create, patent, and launch. In business, the fundamental means of attracting customers to your offer over alternatives is the unique value proposition, or UVP. And your unique value begins with you. It means knowing what you have, cataloging your assets, and finding your IP's unique value(s). Make as exhaustive an asset inventory as you can. Be proactive and figure out your UVP *before* you file a patent, trademark, or copyright.

We touched on idea documentation in chapters 1, 2, and 4 in the don't-do-this-do-that context. Here I'm going to give you the step-by-step process you can begin and finish yourself, from A to Z. By the end of this chapter, you'll have a good idea of how to turn just about any business or product idea into one whose value is so obvious, customers will pay for it without objection. Let's dive in.

Nine Steps to Your IP's UVP

1. Inventory

Before you talk to an attorney, look at your internal and external environment. Inventory everything you and your people have at hand to work with. You may have to coordinate which type of IP protection you apply for and what you choose to manage in different ways.

Many people think they have *an* invention or *a* patent. That's not necessarily *your* invention, and it may not include just *one* patent, either. When I take on new clients, I want to hear about everything they think they have. Often, it's much more than they assume.

My good friend Marissa created a company in the security sector. During our initial call, she said what most potential clients do: "I'd like to file a patent."

I asked more about her company and what she thought made her exceptional. Then we zoomed out not only to the products made, products planned, and services offered but also to the people in her company.

We covered the following questions during the call to inventory her assets. What do your people know? What do you, the inventor or owner or president, know? Where did you come from? What's unique to this opportunity? Why do you think you're exceptional?

Marissa didn't have *one* patent. She had *twelve* patents, including utility and design patents, and other IP rights, including copyrights and trademarks. She also had critical employees and contractors and vendors, including a proprietary relationship with a key vendor whose technology was embedded into every product. That relationship was vital to her UVP.

Sometimes what's unique to you is what other people supply to you because you combine it in a unique way. Apple created a competitive advantage for its iPhone by deploying chips from Intel. Apple also signed an agreement with AT&T to provide cell service. These relationships were part of the iPhone's UVP.

This is the time to examine your contracts with employees, contractors, vendors, and customers. If you look for but don't find those contracts, write them. Fill the gaps. If you don't have an assignment of rights clause for the work they do or the product they build, you don't own it. They might be coming up with inventive solutions with your product or service, so make sure it's yours because you pay for it. Everyone who works with you or for you, even if as a vendor, is contributing to your company in some way.

Decide up front, when it's easy, that you will own what you pay for. Secure the agreement to assign rights first. If you don't have an agreement, and it's still early in the business relationship, get one! It might mean you have to pay the contractor an extra hundred dollars, but isn't it better to own everything?

2. Shift

You can only invent based on what you know. And you can only offer the marketplace value from what you create. And to do that, you may need to stimulate your thinking.

Shift your point of view from yourself ("Is it good?") to the market ("Is it something they will buy?"). Your sales and marketing people are closest to the customers. They know how they'd sell your product. Ask them what they *and* the customers think is valuable about the product.

Get other perspectives as well. Sales and marketing will have a different point of view from engineers, chemists, biologists, and software developers. Understand how they see your product and the value it brings.

Think of patents and trademarks like products you use. Think of where you want to go with these IP assets, what you need them to do, and what you keep as trade secrets (if anything).

3. Align

The best way to get ROI on your IP asset(s) is to make and sell the products or services covered by your IP rights to exclude others—enjoy your limited monopoly. Another way to get ROI on your IP assets is to sell or license your IP to a company with or *without* operating your own company.

Most attorneys treat these paths as if they're identical, but they're not. This is one reason why most patents never make a real commercial impact. You need to know where or *if* there is alignment between your business plan for your IP and anyone else's business.

Know your business model. Research what's happening in your own company if you must. Use primary research by talking with others directly when possible, and use secondary research always. Data provides a different point of view, without regard to initial preconceptions. When we've worked with large companies like Visa, Microsoft, or Apple, we often find a silo effect, with few people knowing what occurs outside their divisions. Even in early stage companies, everybody's so active and busy, they may not be aware of anything outside their offices.

If you're a start-up, it should be easier to determine whether your IP is aligned with the business plan. Ask yourself three simple questions:

1.   How will we use the IP assets—internally or licensing?

2. How and where is the IP aligned with our business today and in the future?

3. Is it aligned with someone else's business?

That last question brings up third parties. As we discussed previously, if you have to litigate to get the attention of your prospective customer, then strategic legal action may be an effective way to attract their notice because litigation demands a response, with urgency. Most of the time, you won't have to sue and don't want to. You don't even have to (and shouldn't) make threats. But think about your bigger competitors—companies (and their competitors) that can acquire you. How would they enforce your IP rights against the others if they bought them (or licensed them)?

What if Google bought your company? Google buys patents in other markets where they have not built their own IP so that they can enjoy the IP rights and corresponding exclusivity. Fitbit had cornered the market in wearables and activity trackers with over 126 patents. Then Alphabet, the parent company of Google, bought them for their operations as well as for their IP rights. It could have just as easily been Apple, who was also interested in the sector, but just like Google, they were later in patent filings than Fitbit (fewer patent filings and with later priority dates). Since there's no second place, if you didn't build those IP rights first, you must buy them.

Other large companies do the same. That's how they get exclusivity. They buy the early innovators and expand the exclusivity over their market footprint, creating more value. You can see how IP rights have a multiplier effect in business.

"But small companies don't have the ability to enforce their patents," many say. You know now that's not true. Most don't ever have to enforce them alone. So build that we-plan-to-enforce-if-needed step into the patent from the beginning. Plan not only for protecting your idea but also for blocking the competition. Can they make a couple of changes and move around you? Why don't they create better assets? Plan for your patent to function in a robust way.

Once someone else owns the market, you can't go back and build a better product later. You have to buy the other company's position. Large companies' distribution and supply chains let them own the market. Before you start tangling with competitors, big companies, and litigation, you need to know your strategy. And that means knowing what you want from your IP.

If you intend to license or sell your IP instead of using it in your own company operations, you must plan for it up front. If you don't, you will regret it. You can invent only from what you know. The more data you see, the more you know about alternatives and how to prevent others from designing around your original idea. This is essential to creating patent assets that other companies will want, or need to license, or buy from you.

Do you want to do the minimum to get started, or DIY, or do you want valuable assets? You can stop at following the USPTO patent application checklist, but you'll likely face rejection and a money pit of office actions. And at the end of the day, your IP is not valuable in and of itself.

Be proactive and do more than the minimum to apply for a patent. Because the minimum you need to *apply* for a patent and the minimum you need to *get* a patent are worlds apart.

When you're sure your IP is aligned with your business plan and strategy, you can look at the context of your market.

4. Research

Earlier in the book, we talked about market research, including patentability research. This is where it comes into play.

Research existing patents and pending applications. Also investigate published research, such as scientific publications, including online presentations.

You can invent only from what you see. The more you see and read, the more you know. Prolific inventors read a lot and research a lot. They identify problems and solutions. It's how they systematically make a lot of combinations.

Consider outside legal support when you're researching patentability. Running the prior art research and finding nothing, or thousands of things, both signal you need help.

Doing the research takes some expertise, because almost no invention is completely new ground. Odds are your invention was derived from something else or had some precedent. It may be a combination of existing features. If so, a patent examiner will always find out.

Finding too much information is like stepping in quicksand. You need someone to pull you out. That's where a patent attorney comes in.

Even if you have done the patentability research yourself, the lawyer should trust but verify. There's no obligation to do the research, but it's worthwhile to create a quality asset. That additional research will increase your likelihood of success.

In one case, a company conducted their own research. Their results? Nothing. We conducted patentability research and analysis and found only a couple of granted patents and a larger number of published pending patent applications. We noted that almost all the patent applications had been abandoned. This pattern was incredibly unusual for any sector. Further analysis showed that they were all filed by independent inventors and start-up companies that were out of business. It was a complicated area, but the company had a solution that worked. We learned what went wrong with the abandoned applications and incorporated the insights into the description of the new patent application for the company.

Nobody can guarantee success, but research gives you the context from which you can differentiate your invention from others. Building that data into your story is essential. Remember: Compare, contrast, and capture. This information will help you fight the patent examiner, because you can't add more details later.

A lot of entities—including a majority of companies—neglect or omit doing the research. Differentiation is not part of their patent. Big mistake. Your UVP and this differentiation from known prior art must go in the initial application to streamline prosecution and increase the likelihood of success in realizing the intended claims for that invention.

Remember, everything has a time stamp. If you add more details later, the new matter gets a new date. Each time you amend your patent, the "fence" gets smaller, and what you have a limited monopoly to isn't as valuable. Eventually it stops being valuable altogether. That's why 98 percent of tech transfer patents don't get licensed.

Most IP law firms don't tell you to research or even ask if you have, because it's not a requirement. Attorneys in general are not businesspeople. They follow the law and do what is required, not what is valuable. Most firms offer no research and no strategy. So you may as well get started with what you can yourself, then bring in the experts.

Even now, this early research will help you shape your UVP. Because when you know what you have, and you know what's around you, you can compare it to and contrast it with others.

5. Compare

In a unique value proposition, the emphasis is on unique. Is your IP as unique and valuable as you thought it was? If so, how? And so what? Your IP may be different from others', but does anyone care?

Answer all these questions with data. Forget your preconceptions and leave all assumptions behind. Look at the trends, at whether your IP really is unique and valuable.

Proximity is a major factor for determining value. Who's in the neighborhood? Which other companies are most like yours? The presence of competition informs the value of your product.

After comparing and contrasting with data to confirm your IP's uniqueness and value, it's time to capture.

6. Capture

Expand your inventory to note more detail. Capture everything that differentiates it from the market. How do you recognize your unique innovation? What makes it valuable? Document *everything*.

Ultimately, this data will be used in patent applications, trademark applications, and trade secret applications. The documentation you've created during the capture phase goes a long way toward proving the worth of your IP.

7. Decide

After the capture phase, decide whether you will create the asset. Just because you've gone this far, it doesn't mean you must proceed.

If you don't have a solid foundation, do not bother. You will waste time, energy, and money creating assets that will never make an impact. No one will care, and no one will pay you for them.

The harsh reality is that your feelings don't matter here. If your patent doesn't offer a significant UVP to your business today and to potential customers or acquiring entities in the future, you should not create the asset—the new product, the new service, the new business. This is why I tell everyone—from students to conference attendees, companies, and investors—that ideas are not assets.

8. Write

If you do pass through this final gate, write down the story of your invention or trademark. Patents have longer stories, but the point stands.

I tell everyone, "Journal!" Pay attention to ideas and document them so that when you inventory, you have a record. Companies often call these records inventor notebooks.

Write first, edit second. Document the concepts, even if they're not fully formed. Don't judge the results. Did you run an experiment? Did it fail? Write it down anyway. Failures matter as much as successes in research. All those failures can be further evidence of uniqueness and value proposition as well as differentiation from prior art. Don't edit them out.

Particularly with patents, tell the story of the problem you're trying to solve and why this unique value is not obvious. Describe all the experimentation involved. Include how your idea compares to others and show why it is the best you know of so far. This should also include how you developed the solution.

9. Hire

Once you've completed the eight previous steps, you're in great shape for an attorney. Yes, you can hire legal help before you decide what you want to do with your invention or what others like it may already exist. Yet the more homework you do up front, the less homework your lawyer will need to do—and charge you for.

Again, some market research can be DIY. Inventorying yourself is DIY. Idea journaling is DIY. Put your sweat equity into it. Give it all you've got until you feel the quicksand we talked about in step four. Then grab the legal helpline you need.

In the next chapter, I'll show you how to contact an attorney who gives you the best chance of securing a patent and bringing your IP's unique value to life.

CHAPTER 12

IP ADVICE: FIND THE RIGHT ADVISORS

By this point in the book, you're familiar with the perils of DIY intellectual property. And I've probably convinced you to get a lawyer for at least a few of the steps to secure your patent, trademark, copyright, and more. In this chapter, I'll show you how to find the right legal help.

Vetting an IP Lawyer

Unlike other attorneys who complete transactional work like contract writing, an IP lawyer is a long-term partner. How long? On average, it's seven to eight years. The typical time from filing a patent to first office action alone can be two years or more. This means that once you file, you may not have *any* sort of interaction with the patent office for at least two years, and any contact you do have will be intermittent. You'll want to make sure your attorney is a good fit for you, as you'll be together for a while.

Every firm should offer you an engagement letter outlining fees and describing the scope of the engagement. Preferably, the engagement letter will also outline the patent and trademark processes, including steps, timing, and expected fees (estimated at least).

When looking for an IP lawyer, reach out to at least three potential candidates. Start with your area and narrow down your search to whomever is easiest to meet with. Many lawyers will offer a free initial consultation. Attorneys who charge a large fee just for a consult ($500+) may be signaling that they are clock-watchers, billing minute by minute; generally, you'd rather have someone who is results-oriented, charging a flat rate for the deliverables. If you're new to IP, then you may need someone who has the disposition of a patient advisor or teacher. Even experienced attorneys may credit their consultation fee toward your subsequent work together. It's important to know the terms from the outset.

When I launched my first practice in the late 1990s, I offered free consultations. Then I realized I was working over forty unpaid hours a week. I decided to charge $100 for a consultation, which was less than my hourly rate at the time. But I was still booking a lot of hours with people who didn't become clients or people who were unprepared to proceed with IP legal services.

So I increased the initial consultation fee again. What I found was that people who are serious about investing in their assets have no problem investing in a consultation. In most cases, I credited my consultation fee toward future work for clients who continued our business relationship, making the consultation effectively free.

My firm does not advertise for new clients. We normally take referrals, and when another business refers a client, we waive the consultation fee outright. The best clients usually come from other clients or from other lawyers or professionals. If you don't know an IP attorney, ask your accountant or corporate attorney, or ask close business contacts.

Don't ask an IP attorney to sign an NDA or wonder if the attorney will keep the consultation confidential. All attorneys have a fiduciary duty to do so. Your attorney is there to help you secure your IP, so don't hold back. Be prepared to tell your IP attorneys about your invention so that they can give you informed advice and guidance on next steps.

I once had an inventor come in for a consultation who refused to explain his invention. At the end of the hour, I still had no idea what it was. To this day, I still have no idea what it was. He had kept it secret for so long, he couldn't bring himself to disclose it—even to an IP attorney. This happens more frequently than you would think; people withhold information because they don't trust the attorney or don't want to share details about aspects of the process that didn't work out. An IP attorney needs you to discuss your invention in detail in order to provide legal advice for the situation.

Lawyers also can't give you their best advice if you show up underprepared. Any IP attorney you meet will have questions for you—and you should, too. Here are eight essential questions to ask at your first meeting.

Eight Questions to Ask IP Lawyers

What's your technical background?
You want to hire a lawyer with solid experience in your specific industry. If you have a pharmaceutical invention, then you want someone with expertise in biotech. Likewise, if you want to patent a new app, you'll need an attorney who has done a lot of work in software.

Our firm's wide array of lawyers has diverse areas of specialization, ranging from high tech to biotech. Some firms do only electrical engineering, or they do only chemistry and biology. You don't want to take a new chemical to someone who specializes in computer science. Only a chemistry specialist will have the vocabulary to help you. Pick an attorney with the expertise to understand your invention and experience with companies like yours. You don't usually need someone with a PhD. If the attorney is experienced in your area of invention with an excellent track record, even if they have a different degree, they may work well with you. Communication is the most essential element of the attorney-client relationship; if your attorney understands you and your disclosure, and has experience in that sector, they may be a good fit.

1. Have you worked with companies like mine?

Think about your company. Are you a start-up company? Are you a fast-growing tech company? Are you raising capital? Are you a publicly traded company? The stage of your business may determine whether a given lawyer is a good fit.

Ask attorneys for profiles of the types of clients they work with. Are any of them like you? Some large firms work only with publicly traded companies and may not serve independent inventors or early stage entrepreneurs. Choose an attorney with experience helping businesses in your current stage and who have the ability to serve you as your business grows.

2. Who will be working with me?

When you hire a law firm, typically you won't *just* be working with one attorney. You'll be working with a team. You need to know them, too. People often presume that going with a large firm is always better, but the bigger the firm, the more likely you are to get shifted to the newest lawyers in that office.

Make sure you know the specific attorney or attorneys with whom you'll be working, and get to know the other team members as well. If possible, meet and talk to everyone who works at the firm. Who will touch your work, and who will do the write-ups? Who will interact with you if you have questions or need something? If there's someone you don't like, go elsewhere.

3.   What is your track record and success rate?

How many of their clients were successful? You can look up this metric on your own. Ethical issues prevent attorneys from claiming a 100 percent success rate. What you want to hear is that *most* of their clients were successful. If they can, ask them to talk about specific clients. *Successful* isn't limited only to obtaining a patent. Your attorney should be able to help you create IP assets that will yield returns within your business or through licensing.

However, past performance does not guarantee future results. That's why patentability research matters. The lawyer must be willing and prepared to do patent research on your behalf, which brings us to the next question.

4.   What will you do to increase my chance of success?

It's not possible to guarantee results. Every application is unique; every invention is unique. The USPTO decides who will be awarded the patent, not the lawyers.

Most of the time, I have a sense of the likelihood of success. I've reviewed hundreds of thousands of patents over twenty-three years as an attorney and as a patent examiner. While I might have an impression after hearing your disclosure, it's still not possible to judge the likelihood of success for patentability without running research on the prior art. After all, that's what a patent examiner will do to judge it.

5.   How do your clients monetize their IP?

Another way to ask this question is, "How do your clients get a return on their investment?"

Attorneys should know how their clients are using their patents. Ignorance of that information is a red flag. You want a patent lawyer with a long-term strategy for helping you in your business.

6. What's the patent process?

In my experience, most aspiring inventors think they just pay a law firm to get a patent. That's not the case. The patent process starts with patentability research and analysis and filing a patent application, but it is an ongoing process and investment with many stages. If you don't ask about it during your consultation, the attorney should tell you about it.

A red flag is if the lawyer wants you to write everything. That's their job. If you're doing all the work, what are you paying for? Some attorneys ask the client to draft the patent application description and then merely reformat it for filing. If you have materials that describe and disclose the invention, provide them. But you should not be charged with drafting the patent application. Ideally, the drafting process is iterative, with good communication between the lawyer and the client.

We always tell people that the first office action is almost always a rejection of the claims filed, as discussed earlier in this book. That's part of how the patent examiners ensure that valid patents are issued, by making initial rejection with prior art discovered in their initial research. It's a process that can be unpredictable, but you need to understand what kind of investment to expect in time, energy, and money at the various stages of the patent process (same for trademarks).

7. How do you charge?

You wouldn't build a house without a cost estimate. When vetting attorneys, find out how much they charge. Ideally, they should offer flat rates. My law firm has always offered flat rates for various patent stages after we understand the complexity of the invention. We can project a reasonable time and effort from there. This benefits the clients because they can budget for the process on a quarterly or annual basis.

If the lawyer offers hourly rates, ask how long your case will take. In complex cases, such as those involving software, a client could spend as much as $25,000 just for filing the patent application, with more costs to follow.

One option is to negotiate a cap. From a business point of view, you're creating an asset. You need to know how to use it, how much it will cost, and what kind of ROI to expect. Setting a budget for attorney fees helps you with this assessment.

Sometimes independent inventors ask the law firm to waive their legal fees because they're just starting a company. Others ask to pay long after the work is finished. These are not reasonable requests when you're trying to create valuable assets for your company. This is one reason most law firms don't work with individual inventors. Be a reasonable businessperson.

Whatever additional questions you may have, don't be afraid to ask them. Get a second opinion or consultation, particularly if the information you have doesn't sound favorable.

I've had to explain to a few of my clients why their idea may not be patentable at the time or at all. It may be painful to hear, but it's far better than spending tens of thousands of dollars for a patent application, only to be rejected repeatedly by the USPTO for years.

As a charitable activity, I extend office hours once a month with High Point University in North Carolina. Students who are entrepreneurial or in the engineering sciences will schedule thirty minutes to ask me questions they would need to ask of a patent attorney. With these clearly structured sessions, students learn from experience what speaking to a lawyer is like.

Students must meet certain requirements to schedule this time. They have to prepare their questions, provide a short write-up of what they want to discuss, and provide research on their topic. Doing this prep work makes our time efficient and productive.

Be like those students. Make the most of your meeting with each attorney, especially if you're on the clock.

Two Questions IP Lawyers Should Ask You

Realize that your attorney is screening you as well. We've turned away clients because we decided they weren't right for us. Here are two key questions they should ask you.

1. What are you going to do with your patent?

If you were to obtain a patent, what role would it play in your company? Are you going to license it, or are you going to build a business? Do you want to make and sell products, or do you just want to sell your patent asset? These are different business models requiring different legal strategies.

2. What research have you done?

No matter which model you plan to adopt, lawyers want to know that you've done your homework. When you go to a patent attorney, bring any market and competitor research you may already have. That information helps a firm decide if they're a good fit for your business and if they have a realistic chance of success when filing your patent.

How to Decide Which IP Attorney to Hire

Now that you've interviewed at least three lawyers, how do you pick the right one? The number one factor is this: Who is most likely to help you create the asset that is useful and valuable in your business?

You need competent representation to create not only a patent but also an asset. We've turned down clients who just want to file cheap, fast patent applications. Quick and dirty filing is often more expensive and less likely to succeed. That's the opposite of creating impact and getting ROI.

The communication factor is a close second. Ask your attorney to include communication free of charge in the engagement letter because clearer communication is better for everyone.

After you've made your choice, remember that it's OK to negotiate. Almost every major company today is prepared to negotiate a cap or flat rate. Some attorneys want to bill by the hour because they don't know how long license negotiations, litigation, support, and other complex tasks will take. However, some firms support trademark litigation, and they negotiate caps and reduced rates.

How complex is your case in relation to others? High tech and software cases tend to involve higher complexity and therefore higher rates. Mechanical inventions should be charged at the lower end of the scale.

Be wary of what counts as billable hours. I hire lawyers to handle corporate matters, securities questions, employment issues, and other areas outside my scope of expertise. I expect to be billed for substantive work. Most of them do not bill me every time I ask a question. I send them substantive work, they do it, and I pay them.

A client of mine had formerly worked with a larger firm. About a year after he'd switched to my firm, the partner from the larger firm invited him to lunch to make an introduction to an investor. The next day, the client received a bill for over $800 for the attorney's time—and his firm was no longer representing the client. When the client asked what to do about it, I encouraged him to let the other lawyer know that it was not a legitimate bill and that he had no obligation to pay it.

Don't make small talk with Big Law because they may bill you for every minute of it. Be clear about what they're billing you for and what deliverable to expect and when. When working with them, keep your own log of billable time.

Be clear on how long each matter should take. With patents and trademarks, the timeline is usually predictable. Expect a delay between the time you file and when you get some information on the filing. Be clear that you want updates when they come in and upon request. You don't know what you don't know. Attorneys have a duty to update you when your case status changes.

You want to establish this understanding up front to account for unforeseen circumstances. If you're working with a solo lawyer or a small firm with only two or three people, find out who the backup is. And be sure that you're working with a professional, accredited attorney who is registered to practice law in your state. You can contact the state bar to inquire if there are any complaints against that attorney or law firm. You can contact the USPTO to inquire about any registered patent agents or attorneys having complaints or other issues. Most sanctions or complaints found valid against lawyers are public record.

I've picked up cases for companies whose attorneys didn't update them. Office actions or correspondence that went to the lawyer wasn't communicated to the client. Their patent applications went abandoned, and they turned to us to try to fix the problems.

If you hear nothing from your attorney after six to eight weeks, for example, make a courtesy request. We like to put the timeline for updates in our engagement letters so that clients have a general idea of how long the process takes. Good lawyers never make their clients sweat.

Be the Best Client

Every business relationship is a two-way street. You'll be working with your lawyer for the next seven to eight years, so you want the relationship to go as smoothly as possible. Be the best client you can be, and your attorney will be the best lawyer they can be.

Don't call them every Friday at 6:00 p.m. about an urgent matter. Don't expect a lawyer to be available 24-7. When urgent issues come up during litigation, communicate them respectfully. Most attorneys will reply to you within two business days. Know what your real questions are. Most importantly, pay your invoices on time.

And if you can help it, don't be . . . *weird*.

Like Pirate Guy. He was weird. At our first meeting, this potential client showed up looking as professional as you'd expect any small business entrepreneur to. His invention sounded credible, with potential for marketplace impact.

When we talked about how much the patent process would cost, he pulled out a picture—and started talking about pirates. He said that if we worked with him on his "billion-dollar idea" and contributed all the patent work for free (of course), we would be given "pirate status" among his crew. Everyone in his company would wear a little skull and crossbones wherever they went. That way, they'd be able to recognize each other. Although now that I think about it, if they're coworkers, do they really need pirate hats and eyepatches to jog their memory? Maybe he hadn't thought that one through. I can't imagine why.

It took more self-control than I'd ever exercised in my life to keep from laughing.

"What do you think?" Pirate Guy finally asked.

"Well," I began, nodding, "I can't say I've ever heard this sort of proposal before."

I explained to him that while we didn't care to engage in pirate behavior, we would be happy to work with him within a traditional, fee-based relationship. He declined.

The difference between Pirate Guy and prolific inventors like Elon Musk is that their unusual worldview exists within the invention itself, not in the business relationship. Be authentic and creative in your work all you like, but don't be crazy about business terms. It's not helpful for business to be wacky. Only the oddest people expect patent lawyers to contribute legal services for free in exchange for something outrageous. Don't be that guy.

Don't be a pirate.

CHAPTER 13

IP ADVICE: DEVELOP A LICENSE AND SELL STRATEGY

L et's say you own a house. Maybe you've lived there for a while, and you're ready to upgrade to bigger views and better space. Or you made an offer on the property because the investment opportunity was too good to let go. Now what? In either case, you could rent the house to a tenant or to a roommate, if you need the extra cash while you still live there. Or you can list the property for sale and be done with it.

You get the metaphor; you can "sublet" your IP with nonexclusive, limited licensing or grant all rights to a buyer—licensing and selling, respectively. We've mentioned this topic here and there throughout this book already, mostly about how *not* to license or sell. What we haven't covered yet is practical how-to. It's time for that now. In this chapter, we will discuss how you can make your IP a valuable asset for others so that they want to pay for a piece of your land—if not for the entire property.

What Is IP Licensing?

Licensing is permission to access your space, to be within your exclusively claimed territory. It can be nonexclusive or exclusive, limited or unlimited, temporary or perpetual. By offering to license your patent to someone, you're saying, "We have exclusive rights that cover A, B, and C. Would you like to pay us to use it?" The same holds true for IP rights.

In the early 2000s, licensing and auction marketplaces connected IP holders to companies eager to license or buy. Even corporations with thousands of employees—and millions budgeted for licenses—found inventors on those websites and sold or purchased patent assets or licenses to them. But like most sites of the early internet, the licensing marketplaces are mostly defunct. Today, if you want a company to license your IP from you, you have to find them yourself.

That's the bad news. It gets worse. Licensing is the hardest way to monetize your IP. Few (if any) will share your passion for and belief in your invention or value your IP rights as highly as you do. Every inventor wants to believe everyone else should want their billion-dollar creation. But you need to convince them that your idea is worth it, and you can't do that without data and evidence.

We'll talk more shortly about how to find companies that might be interested in a licensing deal. My advice to find buyers for your IP is the same, so we'll discuss both together. For now, note that between licensing IP and buying IP, the vast majority of companies who've ever done either have chosen to buy. There are two reasons, the first of which is obvious from the house metaphor that opened this chapter. *If people can afford to buy the house, they'd rather buy than rent.* Companies with money, in most cases, buy IP outright rather than rent it (license).

The second reason buying IP is more attractive than licensing it—again, for most companies—is commercial value. *Just because you own the land doesn't mean it's worth anything.* Years ago, Texas Instruments and IBM both offered licenses to their patents. IBM had over *seventy-five thousand* patent assets at that time in the US alone. Most small to midsize companies found it an insurmountable task to sort through all those patents to find anything they wanted to license, whether or not they were selling a product or service that might be covered by anything.

At IP conferences, I've heard attendees remark that NASA is a licensing success story. It may be true that private companies license NASA inventions and vice versa, but few other research institutions can boast similar performance. In 2008, I spoke at an IP law conference in India. There I learned that India's research university technology transfer success rate is less than 1 percent, meaning fewer than 1 percent of patented inventions ever make it to market via license or otherwise.

There is one more important point to make about licensing IP before we move on to selling. Having an operating company maximizes your chances of successfully licensing your IP. It will be easier to identify potential licensees of an industry if you're in that industry already. Any company would rather sell something that has proven demand than sell anything that the market may or may not want.

Running a business benefits you even more if you'd like to sell any IP your business owns. You can probably guess why.

What Is IP Selling?

You don't have to license your patents. You can just sell them. How does that work?

Some companies buy patents outright. Others will invest in a patent and do enforcement-based licensing or sales. But they want to make sure the patent is worth the investment. What is the quality of the patent? Is it even an asset? Most universities don't license or enforce because their IP does not have commercial value as perceived by the market. The same is often true for small companies with IP portfolios. You have to find the buyer—they do not usually find you.

The easier way, as you might have guessed, is to sell your IP along with the operating company that owns it. Third parties are much more likely to buy patents that come with your customer data, workforce, products, capital, knowledge base, and so on. Bundling patents inside a salable business increases the value of both. This is the multiplier effect we covered previously.

So how do you do it? How do you sell your patents, copyrights, trademarks, and more? The answer for selling and licensing is one and the same. Let's cover that now.

How to License (and Sell) Your IP

If your IP isn't valuable for your company, who will it be valuable for? If you can't identify anyone who will find value in your asset, it probably isn't valuable.

Before you can license or sell your IP, you need to know your context. Here are four sets of key questions to give you the answer.

Who else in your industry has inventive solutions to problems? Who in your industry is paying for patent licenses? These show who values IP.

Who competes with the companies that do have patents? A license to your IP can give them an edge against patent-owning competitors.

Who in your industry is suing each other? Having a patented asset they can license or buy may help them. In a patent infringement suit, if your patent covers the claims by either party, they could resolve the dispute by licensing or buying another patented asset they'll have enforcement rights to. This makes your patent valuable to them.

Recall that litigation in IP is like marketing—it gets the attention of your prospective customers. They have urgency; they must respond to you on a timeline. Some companies, large tech companies in particular, won't pay attention to you unless you know someone high up in the company or unless you sue them. This is enforcement-based licensing. You're enforcing your rights to an asset so that the other party will decide to pay for using it.

Litigation-based marketing takes money and time, but it can yield impressive results. Litigating may not be worth it if the market is too small. If a license is worth less than $50,000, it's not worth it. The exception to this rule is if you have a single competitor in your industry and you want to shut them down.

If you don't have a high-quality asset, you have no chance to enforce and no way to license. Some people want to DIY their patent and think they will be able to license or sell the IP. The hard truth is no one will care.

How close are competitors to your IP rights? How much revenue is impacted?

If another company launches an IP that's close to yours, begin with a friendly letter like we discussed in chapter 7. Show them data that says other companies are active in the same space to create a sense of urgency.

That data is helpful to communicate the value for licensing or buying your IP. It's marketing collateral. Never claim a company is infringing. Never send a letter or email saying, "Cease and desist or pay me." At best, the recipient ignores you. At worst, they file a declaratory judgment, especially in patent owner-unfriendly places like the Northern District of California.

If you *have* to enforce your IP rights but it's not a patent enforcement, and if you feel your IP has been leaked or stolen outright, you may be able to deploy the Defend Trade Secrets Act. This law is invoked, for example, when a key employee leaves to join a competitor that suddenly comes up with a directly competing product or service.

You may have other enforcement options if the competing product substantially impacts your revenue and if there is evidence the competitor has infringed on you. For example, you sign a nondisclosure or nonuse agreement with a company and then present your IP to them. They claim they're not interested, only to launch a product or service that's exactly what you told them about.

Is the product obviously competing with you? Can you produce the emails in which you approached them with your IP? Instead of suing them, it might make sense to contact them with a friendly opportunity, as described in chapter 7.

Use business strategy language if you do reach out with that friendly notice. Try something like, "You're operating in this space. We thought you would be interested in having the confidence of operating with exclusive rights to our intellectual property."

Would that same company consider acquiring you? Does your business have enough value to add to theirs? Approach this scenario from a business development, not a legal, perspective. Present it as a joint business deal or a collaborative project partnership.

You must be persistent and proactive. It's a campaign, not a one-off event. If you go into negotiation playing hardball, there will be no mutually acceptable deals.

Most of the time, you should think of enforcement licensing as a business solution. Fighting should be your last option. Large competitors have in-house legal expertise and huge budgets. You don't want to fight a giant like Apple, even if your company is making $10 million or even $100 million in revenue.

One of my clients owns a company that has a multimillion-dollar valuation. They recently discovered that one of their core features was copied by a prominent social media company. The client said, "There is nothing we can do about it because they will clean our clock. We are better off letting them infringe than risking everything in our business to go after them."

It might be organizational suicide to try enforcing a patent against a social media company with a dozen patents across just one department. Instead of confronting the infringer directly, consider contacting its competitors. Even if it's a smaller company, it may find value in your assets.

As we mentioned previously, before you wage war, consult many wise advisors. Consider law firms that offer enforcement services. They will ask if you have run the numbers. Does your patent have value, or did that other company legally run around you? They'll want to make sure your patents are valid.

If your case is strong, the firm may consider a partial or full contingency payment. However, that option will be less likely if there is only one company in your space.

It's possible to borrow funds for litigation, but you will need to be assessed first. Sometimes experts and tech people must create claims charts to prove infringement. This diligence usually takes months or even years, not days or weeks.

Some companies will fight an infringement case on your behalf. They may partner with you outright or buy your company and its patents and enforce them. Some smaller companies prefer taking the latter approach to avoid being the bad guy. As with funds, this diligence usually takes months or even years, not days or weeks. So be prepared for the long haul if you try this method.

You have many options if a competitor infringes on your IP. But none of them are available if your patents are not high-quality assets, as described in the prior chapters.

Assets or Nothing

The best alternative to threatening a lawsuit is explaining how working with you will benefit the other party. That's also how other companies may choose to license your IP or outright buy it.

If you're an entity of reasonable size and you have market traction, you can focus on resolving any disputes by finding opportunities for both companies to thrive. But you have to focus entirely on the other company's needs. And be ready for the process to take a while.

One of our clients was a vendor for a major telecommunications company (telco). Their software, patents, and trademark inventory were valued at $20 million. They believed they could integrate their assets with big telco and expand its footprint. From the time they thought they had found the right opportunity, negotiations took almost a year longer than they anticipated, but the IP assets proved to be an important factor in the deal—they were a huge multiplier on the valuation for the acquisition.

After the dot-com bust, one early stage innovation company had thirty patents pending, but none had been examined yet. So there were no enforceable rights in their IP, but priority filing dates and content were good. They had customers, revenue, and venture capital investment, but their IP assets had a multiplier effect on their valuation. During the due diligence stage, the acquiring company reviewed the patents and found them to be of high quality. They paid $200 million for the other company and its patents. The deal proved beneficial for the acquiring company *and* for the acquired business.

A third company started a software platform business. Family and life changes made the founder decide to stop seeking venture capital funding and put the working platform on the shelf. After years of persistence through multiple channels, the business is now selling to a group who may monetize their patents through litigation or sale to yet another company.

It doesn't matter that the client's company isn't operating anymore, only that there are many large companies operating in the relevant space covered by the company's patent assets. That makes his IP assets valuable, even without ongoing business activity.

Here's another example. An innovation company with software and hardware offerings and a deep patent portfolio with early priority dates and good claims coverage leveraged patents as collateral for a $15 million line of credit for growth capital. The lending entity made this credit decision because they estimated that they could recover at least *five times* their money by enforcing the borrower's high-quality patents, which were the only collateral for the loan.

Instead of raising money for equity, the borrowing company was acquired by a large corporation that paid off the loan at the closing.

What is the lesson from these four cases? Either you have high-quality patents, or you have nothing. Valuable assets won't guarantee success on their own, but if your patents are low quality, no one will talk to you. And we don't want that.

CHAPTER 14

IP ADVICE: KNOW THY COMPETITORS

To create the most valuable intellectual assets you can for your business, it's not enough to file for patents, trademarks, and other protections. Nor is it enough to continually monitor your staff as they generate new ideas and design new innovations.

To win with IP is the same as winning in business: Watch the competition, and stay multiple steps ahead. When you or your IP attorney gathered patentability data and did the necessary market research, those efforts gave you a broad snapshot of your context at a moment in time.

If you plan to stay in business for years to come (or are selling or licensing to someone else who is), you need to keep a steady eye on competitors' ongoing IP activity. Again, there is no patent police. And there are companies that may infringe without any repercussions.

Don't let that be you. Here is a starter list of questions I advise clients to ask themselves today and answer today as well as in the years ahead.

1. What are your competitors innovating on?
2. Are they filing patents or preparing to file? Look for R&D investments. Listen for peers talking about tech or other patented data.
3. Do they have star players who keep inventing for them? Can you hire them away? Are they pivoting somewhere else? Find evidence of how committed they are to the company.
4. Is it worthwhile for you to create a company or release a product around an IP? What will you invest? Who will your competitors be? How quickly will they be able to compete if you launch?

You're probably wondering how to answer these questions.

Up-to-date patent data are an underused tool for companies to achieve superior industry positioning and greater market share. The result of ongoing research can help you stay ahead of competitors, avoid expensive litigation, and prevent *you* from getting sued.

Here's how that might go. Let's say you're working on an inventive solution, and you've done your patentability research to study the competition. What do you do if you are not sufficiently differentiated from prior art?

The pervasive start-up myth says, "Those who launch first win!" In reality, the second or third company to enter the market often takes full advantage of the opportunity.

The last thing you want to do is ignore this opportunity. In 2004, Raytheon suspected that two former employees had started their own company, FLIR, to compete for contracts that Raytheon wanted. In 2007, FLIR beat out Raytheon for a contract, causing Raytheon to sue them for infringement.

The judge ruled that if Raytheon suspected in 2004 that FLIR was infringing on them but waited three years, then Raytheon leadership did not actually think that FLIR had committed infringement. This delay demonstrated that Raytheon did not have conviction and that

Raytheon decided to sabotage FLIR only once they became a threat to their revenue. Raytheon lost and ended up paying substantial damages.

It pays to know your competition. It doesn't pay if you don't. It pays *them*.

Monitoring your competition may involve consulting chapters 8 and 9 again. Before you litigate, check to see if you will be countersued. Does the company you're considering suing have their own patents that you may be infringing on? If you don't know the answer, you're jabbing a stick in a hole that may be a rattlesnake nest.

Cross-licensing is a good way to resolve a patent dispute. But if you have no high-quality patent assets, the competition will end up taking your cash. Spending $15,000 to $25,000 to create one or more patents beats paying $250,000 or $2 million in a settlement.

Patents are unique assets, and they can be more valuable than cash when you're dealing with competitive licensing. Not feeling like filing a patent is no excuse. If your competitors have patents, you risk exposure to them litigating against you. If you've got nothing to offer, then you have to take a financial hit or shut your company down.

Be as equipped as your competition that *do* have patents. This doesn't mean you need to patent *everything*, of course. You just need to take IP seriously and file what makes sense rather than ignoring or delaying.

You must have IP assets that will be valuable regardless of your position relative to competitors. That way, you can resolve a dispute through cross-licensing, or you can enlist the help of their competitors or a litigation fund.

Know what your competitors are doing with their IP. You can find useful competitive advantages, including knowing how your competitors may be leveraging IP to get an advantage over you.

If you can see which path other companies are on, you can get ahead of them and block them with a patent. If you suspect they are working on a new product or feature that aligns with future markets and growth, but they haven't filed anything yet, you can file first.

First mover advantage applies to IP only. With patents, there's no second place. There is one property, one owner, one position to occupy. Being the first mover to create patent assets gives you that advantage.

CHAPTER 15

IP ADVICE: GET OUT OF YOUR OWN WAY

T he general public assumes the legal profession is all tangibles— law books, courtrooms, attorney's offices, the jury bench. And most law schools teach students that cases are decided based on the law applied to the facts of each case. But that's not it alone. There's an X factor that some attorneys are aware of but don't discuss often publicly: the human factor.

Judges, lawyers, juries, and every person involved in the legal process from start to finish affects the law, in all areas of law practice, from homicide trials to IP infringement. In a patent dispute, remember that whoever files a patent first wins. Even if it's David versus Goliath, and David got there first.

Let me tell you a story. A tiny start-up met more than their fair match in a multinational billion-dollar company. The start-up had registered a US trademark and patents in connection to their business that the big corporation wanted to use. The large company was based outside the US but planned to launch a product domestically with a conflicting trademark, products, and services to our small company.

The corporation tried to file their own trademark application, which was rejected.

We learned that the corporation had planned to make a major investment and consider going public in the US. If they did, it would likely have been infringing on the small company's IP. We offered a reasonable amount for them to acquire the small company's IP assets and continue with their plans. Their outside legal counsel thought it was too expensive and said his client would never go for that—even before asking his client. Our small company successfully kept the giant out of their market, without having to litigate to enforce.

People are always an important factor, and sometimes the deciding factor, *especially* for small companies. You can do everything right, but if the right people are not working with you and fighting for you, you stand in your own way.

Intellectual Property, Important People

The people factor is inseparable from IP because all IP comes from people. The cloud can be a component of an invention; a company can be the patent applicant, but a *person* has to be named as the inventor.

Look at the people who work for you. What do they know? How creative are they when solving problems? Answering your customers' problems with inventive solutions may mean creating new IP. If your employees or contractors aren't participating in the process, you are losing assets. Holding regular invention capture sessions, ensuring that they communicate their inventions and creative ideas, and taking notes can open up a whole new world of IP.

Everyone in your company can invent or create anything, from patentable inventions to trademarkable slogans. But if you don't have the agreements in place that we discussed in chapter 6, especially assignment of rights, your IP walks out the door when your employees leave.

Your customer lists, your trade secrets, how much you charge, and your workflow are all critical to your business. You can use this information to leverage technology, pitch jobs, and turn a profit. People, again, are the source of them all.

How people use IP is also important. You need communication with everyone in your business about your assets. Your people can help you police your own IP by watching the market to identify possibilities for enforcement.

And when it's time to file a new patent, you need to credit the right people, too.

Whose IP Is It Anyway?

It's not unusual to discover that the wrong person was listed as an inventor on patent filings. One of the fastest ways to invalidate a patent application is to list too many or too few inventors or to list the wrong ones.

The inventor might be the person in your company who worked on the project and came up with this new product or service. Listing that person's boss as inventor because he wants credit for the invention will jeopardize the application process.

In one case, we noticed that a patent based on a research student's paper did not include the student's name on the patent application. That omission gave the USPTO reason to say no.

However tempting it may be to throw in the names of people not directly involved in the invention, or to leave out the names of those who were, it will only complicate matters. Credit the right people—no more and no less.

Planning for the End (of People)

Every rock band breaks up. So do most cofounders. Start out assuming partnerships will end. You don't want to be cut out of royalties you earned.

The alternative rock band Gin Blossoms formed in 1987 and rose to prominence in 1992. The lead guitarist, Doug Hopkins, was absolutely brilliant, but he didn't get along with the rest of the band. He battled chronic depression and alcoholism for years. Ultimately the band fired him and denied him over half his publishing royalties and all his mechanical royalties.

Whether you're a musician, an inventor, or a cryptocurrency enthusiast interested in minting NFTs, you may find yourself in a similar situation one day. Be prepared and plan for the end at the beginning.

Most start-ups have between two and six cofounders. Chances are, someone will drop out. What happens if someone isn't pulling their own weight? If you unplug the whole company or break it up, what happens to the IP?

The company must own the assets; it's a multiplier for the business. If you didn't assign the rights to the company, then you have to start over, or you have to figure out a way around the originator.

If you've made any of these errors of omission, it may not be too late to fix them. If you're unsure how, talk to a reputable lawyer who understands intellectual assets.

Once you've sorted out the people factor inside your business, consider how it plays out when doing business with others.

Obnoxious People Don't Last

Do people want to do business with you? Being obnoxious about your assets will kill any possibility of securing a deal. Some people think being highly litigious is a smart approach to business. It's not. The person who's threatening to sue everybody will be taken to court for declaratory judgment. Having only a sword won't help when you need a shield.

Recently, Neo IP had a client pursuing a business licensing and collaboration deal with another company. Decision makers at both companies were getting along well, except the CEO of the other business. He was aggressive and offensive, threatening to sue everyone until he got his exact way. That one person ruined the deal.

Obnoxiousness kills business. Reasonableness attracts it.

How to Be Reasonable (and Know What You Want)

I once attended a patent monetization conference where people with high-quality potential assets networked in hopes of finding connections for licensing, enforcement, and litigation. There I met an inventor with several patents to his name. He had everything we looked for in quality assets—functional technology, prior art differentiation, invention dates, and an industry with numerous competitors.

The inventor wanted help with monetization. He said his patents were "worth billions," but he couldn't answer any of my questions. He didn't know the best- and worst-case scenarios for what he wanted for his IP.

Many people at the conference had also met and talked to this inventor. "He's crazy," one person said. "You'll never get a deal done with him." If you don't know what you want, you can't negotiate with anyone. Again, it's the people factor. There was nothing wrong with his patents. It was the patent holder who held his own creations back. Commercialized, the inventions could have been worth millions, probably not billions. But as is, they were worth zero. And everyone except him realized that.

Ridiculous valuations hurt even inventors who run an already profitable business. I once met the founder of a mobile phone solutions company who was shopping his family of patents around. Several companies booked meetings to license his patents. He asked for $90 million. *Ninety. Million.*

That number had no relationship to real-world value in the market. Given how many other patents also relate to mobile phones, and that they were not the only mobile phone solutions company, such a price was absurd. Nine million dollars would have been more reasonable, especially since the inventor's company was a seven-figure company, not a billion-dollar revenue generator. But the guy stuck to his guns. The result was crickets.

If you don't have data to inform your pricing strategy for selling or licensing your IP, you'll have no way of asking for a reasonable price. A bad deal makes a good patent a bad patent.

The Process Never Ends

The people factor always determines whether deals happen. And you want deals—whether it's licensing your IP, selling it with your business, marketing an exclusive product, or turning an infringing competitor into a joint venture partner.

We began this book talking about ideas becoming assets with the right action. Most businesspeople don't realize they can even build IP assets or that IP applies to their industry. By this point, you likely have the ideas that could be valuable assets. But you—the people factor—are the connective tissue inside your business and within your IP.

Documenting your ideas, registering your IP, and converting that paperwork into high-value assets takes *your* intervention. If you don't start documenting your IP in the first place, it's not worth anything. And when you do, never stop. Continually look for IP. New opportunities and challenges become sources of potential intellectual assets. Identify your advantage in the market and the ways you differentiate your IP from your competitors'.

Celebrate your assets. Draw attention to them wherever you can. Put your registered trademark and copyrights on your website. State that you evaluate and enforce your IP. Have a patent wall in your building where customers can see *all* the patents you hold.

And when you pitch to customers, make sure everybody knows how inventive, innovative, creative, and unique you are (without being obnoxious). This way, you'll draw in more business and add more value to your company.

This IP monetization process never stops, and neither does business. More continuous effort creates more worth, which is most valuable when connected to a living, thriving company. As the business owner or founder, you're in charge of that effort. And if you decide to sell your business, you'll need to show that your assets can be even more valuable in someone else's hands. They can, and they will—if you sell. The good news is that you have time to decide. The better news is that the sale price of the business assets or company, or the valuation of the company at funding or financing by third parties, will multiply the price or value of the business without IP.

Consider this case. A start-up wireless communications company that believed they had proprietary and commercially important technology wanted to raise seed capital to fund additional research and product development. With an initial provisional patent application, the company was valued at less than $10 million for that round of equity funding. After making an inventory of all their ideas and innovations, and after conducting patentability research and analysis, the company filed more than ten new patent applications. Subsequent funding by investors valued the company at more than $50 million before the raise. Additional inventions were captured as their products and services evolved, new technology solutions developed, and new patent applications were filed. Now with more than eighty issued and pending patent applications, the majority of which are enforceable to give exclusive rights (granted patents), and coupled with early revenues, the company was last valued at over $200 million before funding in that round. The IP assets created a significant multiplier effect on the business valuation.

Consider this case. A start-up technology company with industrial applications, founded by a serial entrepreneur, raised initial seed capital from angel investors at less than $15 million valuation before the funding. We helped them create a patent strategy informed by patent data, including Patent Forecast software and visualization. Executing that strategy created a patent portfolio that continues to grow, and combined with prototypes and precommercial activities, the company raised additional capital with a valuation over $100 million. The IP assets were the main contributor to the company's valuation—a huge multiplier from their start-up position.

And yet another case. A company with products in industrial applications developed a new product with advanced features and functionality. They had very few IP assets at the time, as most walked out the factory door daily—the key personnel held the design details in their heads, not documented or transformed into IP. After creating patent and trademark assets, the company's assets—including physical products, equipment, and IP assets—were acquired by a private equity firm, and the new company that bought those assets has already realized at least two times the initial valuation.

To return to the outset of this book, intellectual property law really does apply to you. And that's one of the best breaks you may ever get on your business journey.

Your ideas can have tangible, measurable value when you transform them into IP assets that can multiply your business value.

Now go capture that value.

If you'd like assistance doing just that, I'm here to help. Book a consultation with me or my team at www.neoipassets.com. We'll find out where you are on your IP adventure and suggest your next best steps.

Thank you for reading this book and investing in your business, your ideas, and yourself.

ACKNOWLEDGMENTS

I'd like to acknowledge the wisdom shared by influential intellectual property leaders, mentors, and colleagues. Particularly Ron Epstein, whose global monetization work and his unique point of view regarding intellectual property assets has stimulated many conversations about the worth of intellectual property assets in the US and throughout the world. Also, Ed Rilee, my long-term intellectual property law mentor, has been influential in guiding my thoughts and practice since I first launched my law practice in the late 1990s. Thank you to all clients and team members at Patent Forecast and Neo IP, including past, present, and future.

ABOUT THE AUTHOR

JiNan Glasgow George is recognized worldwide for her expertise in intellectual property. She has spoken about intellectual property in front of the United Nations and has been a featured speaker at intellectual property conferences in India, United Arab Emirates, Italy, France, South Africa, Mexico, and Ghana as well as throughout the United States, including New York City, San Francisco, Chicago, and Miami.

As an inventor, investor, entrepreneur, patent attorney, and former US Patent and Trademark Office examiner, JiNan's background gives her the ability to see intellectual property from the corporate, legal services, and government perspectives—a unique personal view not common in this industry. She is registered to practice in North Carolina, and her technical background includes textiles, mechanical, chemical, and electrical engineering. In addition, she has experience with polymer fiber science, biodegradable materials, composites, biomedical devices, surgical applications, fiber optics, software, blockchain, NFTs, cryptocurrency, fintech, energy, biotech, and pulp/paper science. She has degrees in engineering, law, and theology from North Carolina State University, the University of North Carolina at Chapel Hill, and Duke University, respectively.

Her law firm, Neo IP, is based in Durham, North Carolina. Neo IP serves clients throughout the US and internationally. Neo IP helps innovators transform ideas into assets to make a positive impact in the world. In support of this vision, Neo IP connects innovators to the resources they need to make commercial impact so that they can realize their true worth.

Learn more about her law firm at www.neoipassets.com.

Her software company, Patent Forecast, is also based in Durham, North Carolina. Because investment in patent assets always leads market activity, Patent Forecast software provides data, analytics, and visualization to guide investment diligence, business strategy, and competitive intelligence. Visit www.patentforecast.com for more information.